Genetics and Insurance

Genetics and Insurance

Editors

T. McGleenan
School of Law, The Queen's University of Belfast,
Belfast BT7 1NN, Northern Ireland, UK

U. Wiesing
Lehrstuhl für Ethik in der Medizin,
Eberhard-Karls-Universität Tübingen,
Keplerstrasse 15, D-72074 Tübingen, Germany

F. Ewald
La Federation Française des Sociétés d'Assurances,
26 Boulevard Haussman, F-75311 Paris Cedex 09, France

BIOS

Springer

T. McGleenan *School of Law, The Queen's University of Belfast, Belfast BT7 1NN, Northern Ireland, UK*

U. Wiesing *Lehrstuhl für Ethik in der Medizin, Eberhard-Karls-Universität Tübingen, Keplerstrasse 15, D-72074 Tübingen, Germany*

F. Ewald *Conservatoire National des Arts et Métiers, 2, rue Conté, 75003 Paris, France*

Published in the United States of America, its dependent territories and Canada by arrangement with BIOS Scientific Publishers Ltd, 9 Newtec Place, Magdalen Road, Oxford OX4 1RE, UK

First published 1999

A CIP catalogue record for this book is available from the British Library.

ISBN 0-387-91595-8 Springer-Verlag New York Berlin Heidelberg SPIN 10741446

Springer-Verlag New York Inc.
175 Fifth Avenue, New York
NY 10010-7858, USA

Production Editor: Jonathan Gunning.
Typeset by Marksbury Multimedia Ltd, Midsomer Norton, Bath, UK.
Printed by Biddles Ltd, Guildford, UK.

CONTENTS

CONTRIBUTORS

F. Ewald
Conservatoire National des Arts et Métiers, 2, rue Conté, 75003 Paris, France

G. Hauser
Histology-Embryology Institute, Schwarzspanierstrasse 17, 1090 Vienna, Austria

J. Husted
Department of Philosophy, Aarhus University, Bynging 328, Ndr Ringgade, DK 8000 Aarhus C, Denmark

A. Jenisch
Histology-Embryology Institute, Schwarzspanierstrasse 17, 1090 Vienna, Austria

V. Launis
Department of Philosophy, University of Turku, FIN-20014 Turku, Finland

T. McGleenan
School of Law, The Queen's University of Belfast, Belfast BT7 1NN, Northern Ireland, UK

S. Raeburn
Centre for Medical Genetics, City Hospital NHS Trust, Hucknall Road, Nottingham NG5 1PB, UK

U. Wiesing
Lehrstuhl für Ethik in der Medizin, Eberhard-Karls-Universität Tübingen, Keplerstrasse 15, 72074 Tübingen, Germany

ABBREVIATIONS

HIV	human immunodeficiency virus
AIDS	acquired immune deficiency syndrome
MIRAS	mortgage interest tax relief scheme
HMO	health maintenance organization
OR	ordinary rate
ABI	Association of British Insurers
HGAC	Human Genetics Advisory Committee
NHS	National Health Service
GAIC	Genetics and Insurance Committee
DoH	Department of Health
DNA	deoxyribonucleic acid
PKU	phenylketonuria
HD	Huntington's disease

PREFACE

Those tasked with the drafting and implementation of public policy on genetics and insurance face a testing period in the years ahead. In Europe moratoria have been proclaimed in a number of countries by the insurance industry. Many of these self-imposed restrictions are due to expire around the millenial year. Other states have gone further and introduced legislation in an attempt to curb real or perceived abuses of genetic information by insurance companies. Concerns about the possibility of genetic discrimination are fuelled by reports of hardships in states which place a heavy reliance on the private insurance market for the provision of social goods. The policy debate about insurance and genetics is clearly a complex one. An informed understanding of the issues can only be achieved when crucial conceptual distinctions are clarified. An understanding of the structural differences between life assurance and health insurance is obviously important. Distinctions must also be drawn between risk rating and community rating, between mutuality and solidarity, between notions of equity and equality. Nuances of meaning must be carefully explored before any policy debate can begin. What do we mean by discrimination in insurance? Is it possible to make actuarial decisions without discriminating? What do we mean when we claim that an insurance system should be based on equity? How is this different from equality? What, if any, are the policy implications of such distinctions?

This book seeks to address and unpack these conceptual issues. It is the product of a multi-disciplinary international research effort supported by the European Commission BIOMED II program. Most of the contributors to the work have been participants in the Euroscreen project led by Professor Ruth Chadwick which has been investigating the ethical implications of genetic screening with particular reference to public awareness, commercialization and insurance. The essays in this book have developed primarily from the efforts of a research group tasked with investigating the implications of genetic testing upon the insurance industry. This group, drawn from diverse disciplines, has collaborated for over three years in discussion and analysis of concepts such as risk, solidarity and discrimination in genetics and insurance. The book seeks to offer more than a random collection of writings clustered around a common subject; rather it is an attempt to systematically address and examine some of the conceptual issues at the heart of the debate on genetics and insurance.

François Ewald, in his contribution, examines the concept of risk which is central to both genetics and the insurance industry. Jørgen Husted explores the theoretical basis of our understanding of the concept of solidarity. Discrimination and differentiation are also central to the practice of risk externalization through insurance. Distinguishing between different risks does involve a type of discrimination. Veikko Launis carries out a close analysis of the different understandings of discrimination in the context of genetics and insurance. Urban Wiesing complements this work with an analysis of the practical possibilities of genetic discrimination and examines the distinctions between private and social systems of insurance. My own chapters address the legal principles which currently underpin systems of social and private insurance and examine different possible strategies for regulating insurance and genetics. The book also benefits from the analysis of Sandy Raeburn, clinical geneticist and genetics adviser to the Association of British Insurers. His chapter provides an insight into the development and operation of a system of insurance industry self-regulation based on a Code of Practice. Gertrud Hauser examines the practical operation of a statute-based system of regulation which has been developed in her native Austria. Finally, the book closes with an examination of the possible policy options for genetics and insurance. In our view it makes sense to consider questions of policy only after the fundamental concepts at the heart of the debate have been fully explored. It is through these efforts that we hope to shed some light on a controversial issue which is all too often characterized by conceptual confusion.

Tony McGleenan
Queen's University
Belfast
June 1999

Chapter

1

INSURANCE, GENETICS AND SOLIDARITY

Jørgen Husted

1.1 INTRODUCTION

'One for all, and all for one!' The ideal of solidarity as epitomized in the famous battle-cry of The Three Musketeers encapsulates a much discussed problem in relation to insurance and applied human genetics. Here the ideal seems to separate into its two aspects 'One for all!' and 'All for one!' which ostensibly cannot be practiced together in this context. The problem most pressingly comes to the fore in relation to individually underwritten insurance – life, health, critical illnes and disability insurance. If the applicant has undergone genetic testing – either for direct treatment or preventive purposes or as part of a genetic screening population program – there exists genetic information on this individual and the question is whether this information should be shared with the insurer. The most pressing issue is the use of genetic tests yielding *predictive* information, i.e. that indicates a predisposition to a disease that has not yet occurred, and not the use of tests that are diagnostic of conditions that have already developed. The question of allowing or denying the insurer access to this new kind of predictive information is what gets the ideal of solidarity into a bind.

'All for one!' If a musketeer is in distress the other musketeers rush to his aid lending him all their strength. For a given group or community the ideal of solidarity implies the obligation to stand by those members who need help. If the insurer is allowed access to predictive genetic information this will make it possible to identify applicants who are especially vulnerable and thus either claim forbiddingly high premiums or render them directly uninsurable. So, allowing that access would clearly violate the 'All for one!' aspect of solidarity. A musketeer who is more likely than the rest to end up in distress is simply abandoned to his fate as a 'bad risk'. So much for solidarity!

'One for all!' Whereas the first aspect of solidarity lays down the obligations of the group or collective towards its individual members this second aspect deals with obligations in the reverse direction. Each member of a group characterized by solidarity has to contribute his share to make the unity viable. Just as the group is obliged to *stand by* needy individuals the individual is obliged to *stand together* with the others. If a member tries to gain the benefits from the solidarity without putting in his own share like the rest, the group cannot accept this free-rider without violating its own spirit of solidarity. To maintain solidarity, the group has to insist that each member joins and participates in 'utmost good faith'. Thus, in the insurance context, the insurer has to insist that the applicant gives full access to all predictive information known to himself. Otherwise the applicant's risk status and hence his proper contribution to the collective enterprise of standing together cannot be determined. So much 'utmost good faith' and its consequences for the sharing of information has to be demanded in the name of solidarity.

Usually, solidarity works both ways as in the musketeers' case. However, in the case of individually underwritten insurance of the relevant kind it cannot go both ways, at least not in the same way as with the musketeers. Here the demands of 'standing by' and 'standing together' seem to be incompatible after the loss of 'genetic innocence' and consequently of 'mutual genetic ignorance'. A choice has to be made. As is well known, some jurisdictions have chosen – in the very name of solidarity – to refuse insurers access to predictive genetic information. And as is also well known, the insurance industry is vehemently opposing this – also, indeed, in the name of solidarity. Each side argues that unless its own proposal is upheld the ideal of solidarity is empty.

To get out of this impasse one has to recognize that solidarity is an equivocal term with different core senses. With a view to sorting out some of the underlying problems the following offers a brief survey of the more important meanings of solidarity and, on this backgroud, a discussion of the insurance issue.

1.2 THE MANY FACES OF SOLIDARITY

First, a basic distinction can be made between the two basic meanings of solidarity. On the one hand there is what may be called *communal solidarity*; this is solidarity as practiced by a group of people *having a common interest*. On the other hand there is *constitutive solidarity* as practiced by a group of people *having an interest in common.* As is to be expected each of these meanings gives a distinctive content to the ideal of solidarity.

1.2.1 Varieties of communal solidarity

In all instances of this kind of solidarity the groups are already defined or constituted by a common interest and solidarity is practiced in the name of this interest. However, the interest can figure in different ways.

Group solidarity. Here the common interest is the cement or organizing principle of the group and the members have a common interest in the sense that what is good or harmful to this interest is (or, at least, perceived to be) good or harmful to the individual too. Typically, people have a common interest in the relevant sense by *belonging* to the same organized unit X, where X may be an ethnic minority, a profession, an occupation, a creed, a unit of organized labor, local community and so forth. The group's practice of solidarity by standing by its weak and needy members is a case of 'looking after one's own'. While individuals in need, of course, receive help for their own sake, it is also very clear that solidarity is being practiced for the sake of the common interest. By recognizing its collective responsibility towards its needy members the group secures the loyalty of all members to the common cause and thus, also in this way, promotes it. In the same way the group is able to make legitimate demands on the individuals to contribute their share to the lifting of the burden of the collective responsibility.

Moral solidarity. These are instances of communal solidarity where solidarity is not, or only to a low degree, practiced for the sake of the common interest but solely for the sake of the needy individuals benefiting from it. Also, solidarity is not practiced as a collective responsibility, but as an individual moral responsibility. The common interest is not that of belonging to the same organized unit but the perception of a bond between individuals: a fellow-feeling or a sense of sharing a common lot and recognizing oneself in the other. The basic principle behind this kind of solidarity is 'making the other person's cause one's own' out of a sense of duty. The more prominent varities of moral solidarity are as follows:

(i) Brotherhood solidarity. An example is where women in so-called developed countries out of a feeling of sisterhood support, e.g. financially, politically or morally, women in other cultures who are deemed to be oppressed, or when organized labor movements try to help unorganized laborers in other countries.
(ii) Charitable solidarity (neighborly love or philanthropic solidarity). Here people give help to needy people out of the feeling that they should do unto others what they would want these to do unto themselves if they were in their situation.

(iii) Social solidarity. The acceptance of well-off citizens of income redistribution in order that the poor and needy might be helped by the state 'We are all in the same boat!'
(iv) Egalitarian solidarity, as is known in the kind of European health care systems that operate under the principle of 'free and equal access'.
(v) Humanist solidarity, e.g. humanitarian aid in the event of natural disasters or ethnic cleansing, or an individual's joining a war against forces that oppress other individuals. This brand of solidarity and its underlying feeling of a bond between all human beings is eloquently expressed in John Donne's famous poem:

> No man is an *Island*, intire of it selfe;
> every man is a peece of the *Continent*, a part of the *maine*;
> if a *Clod* bee washed away by the *Sea*, *Europe* is the lesse,
> as well as if a *Promontorie* were, as well as if a *Mannor*
> of thy *friends* or of *thine owne* were;
> any mans *death* diminishes *me*, because I am involved in *Mankinde*;
> And therefore never send to know for whom the *bell* tolls;
> It tolls for *thee*.

Moral solidarity is a response to moral duties, not to group-membership duties. It is, typically, the individual him or herself who recognizes the duty and determines the extent of solidarity.

1.2.2 Communal solidarity and collective health insurance

The history of health insurance in a number of European countries offers an interesting illustration of these concepts. Collective financing of health care started out from instances of group solidarity. The predominant principle was *mutuality* or *reciprocity* understood as mutual support among members of organized groups sharing a common interest (professional, occupational, local community). Mutual benefit funds were created where the members shared the cost of medical expenses for the ill and needy among them. Typically, everyone at a given level of income paid the same amount, premiums being identical for young and old, healthy and unhealthy, individuals with low or high risk. In this way the 'mutualist' insurance schemes regulated individuals' contribution by a principle of equality: the individual's contributions being determined by income status irrespective of risk status. To various degrees the funds practiced solidarity in the sense that not only did healthy members support members with health problems according to 'I scratch your back and you'll scratch mine!' but some members of the common-interest group – the poor – gained, by virtue of the common fund, access to a level of health care that their own income would not have given them access to. The members with the higher income level thus accepted that they themselves in case of illness got less help so that these poor people could be helped to secure access to a 'decent minimum of health care' (often far less than the level reserved for members contributing from higher income levels). This characteristic made solidarity into more than just mere reciprocity. In the second half of the twentieth century public health care schemes replaced the mutual benefit funds. This has meant a clear shift from group solidarity to moral solidarity under the slogan of 'equality in health care'. When national governments took over the organizing of solidarity in this area, *egalitarian solidarity* thus became the dominant ideal as summed up by the words, 'From each according to his ability, to each according to his need'. This gave rise to the principle of income-related contributions and equal utilization entitlements for all, that is irrespective of the amount they contributed. By enforcing a certain amount of income redistribution the public health care programs aim to achieve *equity* and *equality* in health care: equity being the principle regulating contributions (same income, same contribution, higher income, higher contribution etc.) – or, in other words, everyone contributes *the same*, meaning the same proportion of his or her income or ability to pay – and equality being the principle of access: services are not delivered according to ability to pay but according to need.

1.2.3 Varieties of constitutive solidarity

In its most common everyday use 'solidarity' is probably taken to mean some form of communal solidarity. In certain contexts, however, there is a well-established use with quite a different meaning of what is here termed 'constitutive solidarity' (or alliance solidarity). As already mentioned the prime difference between the two kinds of solidarity is the difference between the situation where a number of individuals share a common interest and the situation where a number of individuals have an interest in common. In the latter case the individuals may realize that the best way to promote their individual interest is to join with the others to set up some kind af collective unit, the unit being constituted by a form of contract laying down the conditions for the individual's contribution to the collective endeavor as well as for the individual's benefiting from it. A well-known example of this is when individual workers join to form a union. Each worker has the same interest as the next one, namely to be able to earn a decent living by selling his labor to an employer. As each worker, however, realizes that on his own his negotiating position vis-à-vis the employer is very weak – since the employer may be able to find another worker who is willing to accept lower wages – the thought of solidarity as 'standing together' in a common front vis-à-vis the employer strongly suggests itself:

> Solidarity for ever . . .
> Solidarity for ever, for the Union makes us strong.

> When the Union's inspiration thru the worker's blood shall run,
> There can be no power greater anywhere beneath the sun;
> Yet what force is weaker than the feeble strength of one,
> For the Union makes us strong (R. Chaplin, 1900)

Inspired by this ideal of solidarity – 'One for all!' – the workers set up a union to further their individual interests. To make the union work each member has to contribute in a specified way – by paying a fixed amount of their wage, refusing to work for an employer who does not recognize the union's right to negotiate collectively on behalf of the workers, joining, if necessary, in industrial action. What is being appealed to in Chaplin's song is solidarity in this constitutive sense, the necessity for workers to make an alliance as the only way to secure or promote their individual interests. Of course, once the union is established as a going concern, the workers now have an interest in common – the union – and they may now want to appeal to communal solidarity, e.g. in discussions of whether and how to support weak members – 'All for one!' – or other workers fighting for their rights.

Another well-known example of constitutive solidarity may be called *entrepreneurial* solidarity; this is the case where a number of individuals get together as stockholders to establish a company, with the goal of the individual of increasing his or her capital. It is also the case where some individuals, e.g. farmers in a local community, create a cooperative enterprise, e.g. a cooperate dairy or farming-machine pool, to promote their individual interests. In these instances, again, the collective unit is created by a kind of contract defining the terms for the individual's contributions and benefits. The typical principle for entrepreneurial solidarity is that the individuals receive benefits (or have to accept losses) in proportion to their individual contribution (stocks bought or milk delivered). Furthermore, in entrepreneurial solidarity the members are said to be economically responsible *in solidum*: they stand (or fall) together in the sense that they are jointly and severally liable or responsible.

Constitutive solidarity in the form of entrepreneurial solidarity is also known from health insurance, i.e. private health insurance. Here it is often called 'risk pooling' which refers to arrangements for collective financing of health care costs, and in which – so to speak at the end of the day – people who enjoyed good health through a given period have financially supported people who have been ill and used health-care services. However, the 'healthy' members of the scheme have not given their individual contributions over the years in order to support the 'unhealthy' ones, but solely in order to receive a benefit for their own individual interest, namely security in the face of uncertain risk. Also, in risk-pooling, the principle for setting up the arrangement and determining the individual's contribution is not related to individual ability to pay but depends on the applicant's health status (degree of risk). In spite of these characteristics that clearly go against the spirit of solidarity known from health-care schemes in the form of communal (viz egalitarian) solidarity, health-care arrangements of the entrepreneurial variant are, nevertheless, often said to practice solidarity. What is meant by 'solidarity' here is of course not the notion of the strong lending their strength to the weak, but rather the idea of individuals that have an interest in common getting together to share burdens and benefits in the face of uncertain risk. This is solidarity in the constitutive sense, as is also made very clear by the principle of organizing this kind of standing together; it is the principle of *equity*, in this context not having the meaning of equal contribution (income-defined equity), but laying down 'that the contribution of individuals should be approximately in line with their known level of risk' (risk-defined equity).

Finally, as constitutive solidarity in the form of entrepreneurial solidarity is the very core of private insurance of all types, this is also what is meant by solidarity in the context of individually underwritten insurance for life, critical illness, etc. As the idea behind this kind of insurance is constitutive solidarity, and as solidarity in this sense requires the complementary principle of equity in the sense just specified, there can be no question that this kind of insurance – in the very name of solidarity – has to insist on the insurer's right to perform an individual risk evaluation or risk discrimination for the applicant, and thus that the applicant should be required to share – 'in utmost good faith' – with the insurer any kind of risk-status relevant information, e.g. the results of genetic tests.

1.3 SOLIDARITY VERSUS SOLIDARITY

The problem and tensions involving insurance, genetics and solidarity may now be described as follows. On the one hand, many European countries have created, or are in the process of creating, egalitarian health-care systems based on solidarity, meaning income-related contributions and equal utilization (need-defined equality) for all irrespective of the amount they have contributed. Health care is considered an important social good, not a market commodity, which can be bought and sold in the open market, and the equality of access is considered a central social value. Creating that situation has taken a lot of hard work and it is being considered all important to uphold its principles and their strong support in the population and thus to defend the ideas against any form of erosion. The system covers all and everyone and any attempt to exempt some individuals generates great debate. As is well known, there have been discussions as to whether people who have self-inflicted illnesses or disabilities due to lifestyle, e.g. cigarette smoking or hazardous sports activities, should be taken out of the coverage and be left to insure themselves, at least against certain eventualities. Here the discussion is possible because these kinds of health problems can be seen as belonging to the individual's own area of control. However, even discussing a proposal to deny a person coverage on account of his or her genetic make-up would be quite unthinkable. A person's genetic make-up is a lot drawn in the 'genetic lottery' and thus wholly outside individual control; genetic factors are surely not one's fault or under one's control. Discriminating against individuals on that account would obviously be a case of morally indefensible discrimination. The very idea of the system would fall apart and egalitarian solidarity, in this essential area, would exist no more.

On the other hand there are the schemes of private insurance. They, too, are open to all, and the regulating principle is again equity, however this time risk-defined equity. Thus, risk-discrimination is the basic modus operandi of the industry; without information needed to estimate risk there can be no risk classification, and without risk classification, there can be no private insurance. The project of creating a group of people sharing the burdens and benefits in the face of an uncertain risk requires the design of a workable risk-sharing formula. 'A risk is a risk is a risk', and any attempt to make exemptions for some kind of risk factors, e.g. genetic factors, would be wholly unacceptable as viewed from the very idea of private insurance. Also, it would be quite arbitrary, and thus grossly unfair, to make exemptions in the case of some individuals with a considerable risk, namely a serious genetic risk factor, while claiming higher contributions from applicants with a 'traditional' one; that would mean punishing some applicants for *their* kind of risk while favoring other applicants. The very idea of the system would fall apart, if this difference of treatment were to be insisted on by legislation; it could no longer be described as a private insurance system. Futhermore, such a proposal endangers the insurance industry and thus all the persons who have a special interest, even need, in joining a solidarity scheme of that kind. Legal prohibition of the use of genetic information during the underwriting process would be likely to result in premium increases that place insurance beyond the reach of many people, particularly those already least able to afford coverage – at worst, it could threaten the financial solvency of the insurance industry. Finally, a prohibition on the sharing of genetic information would create great problems for insurers under the heading of 'adverse selection', where individuals with high genetic risks take out large insurances from insurers who are being kept in the dark [1].

So, on the one hand the state, at least in many European countries, strives to uphold its all-important ideal of solidarity and thus may end up with a prohibition meant to make it impossible for insurers to discriminate against individuals on account of their genetic makeup. On the other hand the insurance industry strives to uphold its principle of solidarity insisting on the need to design a workable risk-sharing formula in all cases of risk-pooling. As solidarity here clashes with solidarity the question is whether solidarity, as correctly understood, is able to offer a resolution.

1.4 AN IMPASSE

Consider again the contention that people who are genetically disadvantaged should have access to insurance on the same terms as the genetically advantaged. This is argued for in the name of (moral) solidarity. Initially, it also seems quite acceptable that individuals who are already disadvantaged should not – and indeed for that very reason: their unfortunate lot – be put to further disadvantage, but should instead receive some kind of support from the advantaged. The problem, however, is to make the argument from solidarity work to show why in the insurance context this kind of solidarity should be practiced and thus allowed to demand exemptions from the traditional practice of solidarity in insurance.

First, it could be argued that the refusal to put the genetically disadvantaged at further disadvantage is in line with principles that people are already committed to in the insurance context. Thus S. Gevers argues: 'In the past, many genetic risks which could not be detected have been insured without making a difference beween individuals. Why would it be unfair to maintain the until now existing solidarity between insureds . . .?' (Gevers, 1993, p. 132) The answer, of course, is that 'the until now existing solidarity between insureds' is a kind of constitutive solidarity. The sole reason why in the past many genetic risks were insured without making a difference between individuals is not the practicing of any kind of moral solidarity but is precisely that those risks could not be detected and thus could not be used for setting up an equitable risk-sharing formula. Now, or in the future, when these risks can be detected 'the until now existing solidarity between insureds', i.e. constitutive solidarity, requires that they are taken into account on a par with other kinds of risk.

Secondly, as it seems unfair that people who are already disadvantaged should be put at further disadvantage the fair distribution of costs and benefits requires that the genetically disadvantaged should have insurance offered on the same terms as the advantaged. However, as the following quotation from an editorial in *Nature* (1991) insists, this seemingly quite acceptable 'should' points to another and more problematical 'should': 'The contention that people unlucky enough to carry identifiable genetic abnormality should not be denied insurance on the same terms as other people begs the question why people relatively free from identifiable genetic abnormality should therefore pay more than would otherwise be necessary.' Requiring that the genetically disadvantaged should have access to insurance on the same terms as the advantaged is the same as requiring that the advantaged should pay more than otherwise necessary. Now it may very well be that the genetically advantaged would *want* to pay more than would otherwise be necessary in order to better the position of the genetically disadvantaged but the question as the editor of *Nature* makes clear, is whether they *should* pay more than necessary. And the argument that they should do so in the name of solidarity and the fair sharing of costs and burdens fails entirely. The kind of solidarity that the insureds are practicing is precisely such that the premium 'that would be otherwise necessary' *is* the individual's *fair and equitable* contribution under a risk-sharing formula worked out according to the principles of actuarial fairness and taking account of all relevant risks. Although it would be laudable if they chose to pay more than their fair contribution in order to help others it would be quite unfair to demand that they pay more than fairness requires.

A reaction to this last point could be that moral solidarity should be allowed to overrule constitutive solidarity, and thus its notion of fairness, as practiced between insureds. The reasoning would be that the existence of an especially disadvantaged group of individuals requires some kind of special consideration and exemption from the standard risk-sharing procedures. In such cases moral solidarity should overrule constitutive solidarity and its implication in insurance, namely insurance discrimination that means putting already disadvantaged persons at further disadvantage. To this argument M.A. Hall gives the following answer, '. . . this argument against insurance discrimination is not unique to genetics. It would apply with equal force to any source of personal misfortune over which one has no control, including being hit by a truck. And, it applies to sources of misfortune that we think are wrong to penalize, such as working in high-risk occupations or living in high-risk neighborhoods. This is an argument, in essence, that private insurance should be abolished and replaced with social insurance schemes that pool all or most risks across society. This argument carries far beyond genetic discrimination; it points toward flat community rating, barring the use of virtually any risk information.' (Hall, 1996, p. 17) Thus, again, the argument from solidarity fails to achieve its end. If moral solidarity should be allowed to overrule constitutive solidarity in the case of genetic discrimination and there is nothing unique about the position of people with this kind of disadvantage vis à vis people with other kinds of disadvantage, then the very principle of private insurance is totally eroded.

The last remaining way out to make it possible for genetically disadvantaged people to have access to insurance on the same terms as others seems to be an *appeal* to solidarity in this special case of insurance discrimination. Thus a *Lancet* editorial (1996) asks whether society might be willing to restrict genetic information to direct medical uses and 'forego any premium advantage in being able to show that we are genetically at risk'. In his discussion of this R.J. Pokorski envisages an eventuality where an insurer agrees to accept everyone at risk of a serious disease with the stipulation that (i) the premium would be the same for everyone regardless of risk and (ii) genetic test results – favorable or unfavorable – could not be used to either increase or decrease the premium. Such a plan would clearly incorporate a form of moral solidarity into the constitutive solidarity of insurance and would no doubt be welcomed by those with an unfavorable test result. Pokorski argues, however, that it has no chance of success as the appeal to solidarity is up against mightier forces; people with negative genetic test results would never accede to such an arrangement however laudable it is from the point of view of moral solidarity. He offers the following forecast of the scheme's foundering, 'Genetic testing will be readily available in doctor's offices and free-standing commercial laboratories and, eventually, via home testing, and people will learn that risk conferred by genetic characteristics spans a range from low to high, with most individuals having an average risk. If confronted with de facto subsidization by regulations or professional codes of conduct that forbid sharing of information except when it confers a financial advantage, applicants who know they have neutral or favorable genetic profiles will insist that insurers use this information to grant lower premiums. Consumer purchasing decisions are not governed by utopian percepts, but by rules established in perpetuity, namely to maximize personal financial gain. Harsh as it may sound to the ears of a society that subscribes to egalitarian principles, solidarity ends with a negative genetic test.' (Pokorski, 1997, p. 213)

So, once again, the argument from moral solidarity will not work in the context of insurance. It may carry weight enough to make the populace decide to endorse a system that calls for significantly higher premiums to subsidize others at greater risk but in the end, Pokorski contends, the utopian ideal of moral solidarity will not be able to withstand the individual's interest in maximizing his or her own financial gain: ' . . . these issues will not be resolved by legislative fiat or organized efforts within the medical community to restrict access to information. They will be decided by the consumers. In the end, people will vote 'with their feet,' i.e., they will choose a solution that most closely meets their needs' (Pokorski, 1997, p. 212). As long as private insurance remains private insurance it goes along by its own rules and rationale and in this context there is no durable foothold for moral solidarity.

1.5 BEYOND SOLIDARITY

The moral intuition that people who are already disadvantaged, in this case genetically, should not be put to further disadvantage and denied access to insurance on the same terms as others cannot, it seems, be upheld by an argument from moral solidarity. It appears quite arbitrary to try and make a special case to show solidarity with persons who are genetically disadvantaged. As Pokorski remarks, 'For example, if there were an increased but virtually identical likelihood of early claim in two 40-year-old applicants, and the risk was genetic in one person and nongenetic in the other, prohibiting use of genetic information would mean that only the individual with nongenetic risk factors would be required to pay additional premiums.' (Pokorski, 1997, p. 212). And furthermore, to make the situation even more unfair, the person with nongenetic risk factors would be forced de facto to subsidize the applicant with the same level of risk but due to genetic factors.

As moral solidarity cannot be used to plead the case for the genetically *disadvantaged* there only remains the possibility of pleading their case as the case of *genetically* disadvantaged individuals. But how can *the kind* of a person's disadvantage be morally relevant? In private insurance or risk-pooling, as we have seen, *any* kind of disadvantage is relevant and has to be taken into account in setting up the risk-sharing formula. In social insurance, on the other hand, for example in the egalitarian health care systems, *no* kind of disadvantage is relevant and every kind of risk is equally covered. In order to answer this question it first has to be realized why the argument from moral solidarity fails in the context of insurance. The argument, and thus the attempt to gain endorsement in the insurance context of the fundamental value of egalitarian risk-sharing schemes, fails because what is being appealed to as the fundamental value – moral solidarity – is actually not the fundamental value at all.

Egalitarian health-care systems practice, or strive to practice, moral solidarity. This practice of moral solidarity is, however, aimed at manifesting a deeper-lying value, namely equity understood as equality of treatment based solely on need. Equity as serving people's needs in an equitable manner is one sense of 'equal consideration' and points to another sense of it, namely equality, specifically egalitarian equality, that is the general aim to 'make people more equal', also when direct need is not in question. Furthermore, this ideal of egalitarian equality has two dimensions, creating equality in respect of opportunity, i.e. equality in starting and running conditions of people's leading their lives, and equality in respect of outcome. As is well-known, the proper interpretation and balancing of these two dimensions are a standing source of debate on how to implement egalitarian health-care systems.

Thus, underlying the *practice* of moral solidarity in egalitarian health-care systems is an ideal of equality demanding both that people are being treated as equals and, in certain important respects, are 'made' more equal. Nevertheless, just as moral solidarity is not a fundamental value neither is equality. The point of the ideal of equality is not to cherish and promote a certain factual property of people – their being equal – for the simple reason alone that as a matter of fact people *are* not equal. The point of the ideal of equality is to uphold and try to manifest in social practice the fundamental value of each individual human being – the idea that each human being has worth or value in him or herself. Another way of expressing this idea is by saying that human beings have the same or equal worth or that it is intrinsically, objectively, and equally important that any human life flourishes rather than founders and, above all, that it not be wasted. The crucial concept, however, is not equality but *individual worth* or, in Kant's terms, that human beings individually have *dignity*. Now, this idea of human worth, and thus of the equal worth of individual human beings, amounts to a principle *prescribing* how human beings *are to be treated*, namely that each human being is to be treated with the kind of respect and concern that expresses the recognition of him or her having fundamental value or being an end in him or herself. This principle is called the principle of respect for persons or of respect for the individual. One aspect of it is the demand of *equal* respect and concern for all that manifests itself in egalitarian principles and social practices, equality, however, being a derivative value, namely subordinated to individual worth or dignity.[2]

If this is right, it can now be suggested that what underlies the moral intuition about how to treat the *genetically* disadvantaged in the insurance context is not moral solidarity or equality but the idea of human dignity and the principle of respect for the individual. The thought behind the moral intuition seems to be that insurance discrimination on the basis of genetic factors, favorable or unfavorable, poses a threat to, or directly violates, these fundamental ideas. And if it is those ideas, and not solidarity, that are at stake, the situation of course changes radically. Harking back to Pokorski's forceful argument some new points may now be made. First, there is his forecast that the resolution of the insurance problem rests with consumers and that people in the end will vote 'with their feet' and choose a solution that most closely meets their needs. To this it can now be pointed out that in many European countries people have and are voting with their ballot papers to create egalitarian health-care systems in order to secure equal respect and concern for all. Secondly, there is his contention that 'consumer purchasing decisions are not governed by utopian percepts, but by rules established in perpetuity, namely to maximize personal financial gain'. Here it is relevant to point out that as a matter of fact many, and perhaps even more and more, consumer purchasing decisions are definitely not governed solely by the aim of maximizing personal financial gain. When there are higher values at stake, e.g. animal welfare, ecology, environmental preservation, human rights, preservation of traditional lifestyles, many consumers choose differently from what would be dictated by the aim of maximizing personal gain. This goes for buying eggs, beef, motorcars, potatoes, television sets, coffee, package tours etc., so there is no reason why it could not also become a relevant dimension in insurance purchasing decisions. If one kind of insurance scheme is seen as an affront to the idea of human dignity, and the other not, that difference could easily become a decisive factor swinging public opinion and preferences in favor of the latter. Finally, Pokorski's statement, 'Harsh as it may sound to the ears of a society that subscribes to egalitarian principles, solidarity ends with a negative genetic test' now gets a new answer. If it is a matter of showing solidarity Pokorski may very well be right; why should insureds forego lower premiums in order to subsidize genetically disadvantaged applicants but not applicants having other kinds of disadvantage? However, if the genetically blinded insurance scheme is not designed to – arbitrarily – subsidize people with a special kind of disadvantage but instead to uphold the idea of human dignity it is not at all clear why a negative genetic test should put an end to people's commitment to its principles.

So, in the end, it all comes down to the question whether insurance discrimination using genetic information on individuals goes against the ways of treating individuals that are demanded by the idea of human worth or dignity. Recent history tells us a very frightening story of misuse of genetics and appalling disrespect for human beings; however, also recently, the new medical genetics has found ways of benefiting people, both in a preventive and a therapeutic way, by utilizing genetic discrimination. In spite of the understandable apprehension about genetic discrimination this latter development has made the practice of it *in the medical* context acceptable because it is beneficial for the individual and takes place within an environment dedicated to the principle of respect for the individual. The proposal to give the private insurance industry access to the results of medical genetic discrimination is a proposal to bring these findings into an environment that does not operate under the principles of beneficence and respect for the individual. So, the question that does not demand the very greatest attention – albeit, of course, rather great attention – as long as genetic discrimination is confined to the medical world now seems to demand this very kind of attention for many years to come. Is there a conflict between the practice of genetic discrimination and the idea of human beings individually having dignity? Actually, the question is not whether there is such a conflict as analyzed from one or other theoretical perspective, but whether people *perceive*, or will come, after proper discussion and reflection, to perceive that there is such a conflict. It is with this eventual perception of things deeply normative, not in legislative fiat or consumer choices that the final resolution rests.

NOTES

1. These possible consequences for the insurance industry are discussed in Pokorski, 1997, p. 207 and p. 212.
2. For further elaboration *vide* Downie *et al.*, 1990, pp. 160–64 and Dworkin, 1996, pp. 42–44.

REFERENCES

Downie, R.S., Fyfe, C. and Tannahill, A. (1990) *Health Promotion: Models and Values*, Oxford University Press, Oxford.

Dworkin, R. (1996) Do liberty and equality conflict? In: *Living as Equals* (ed. P. Barker), Oxford University Press, Oxford, pp. 39–57.

Editorial (1991) *Nature* **352**: 11–13.

Editorial (1996) *Lancet* **347**: 133.

Editorial (1996) *Nature* **379**: 379.

Gevers, S. (1993) Use of genetic data, employment and insurance: an international perspective. *Bioethics* **7**, 2/3: 126–134.

Hall, M.A. (1996) Insurers' use of genetic information. *Jurimetrics J.* **37**: 13–22.

Pokorski, R.J. (1997) Insurance underwriting in the genetic area. *Am. J. Hum. Genet.* **60**: 205–216.

FURTHER READING

Figueras, J. and Saltman, R.B. (1996) On solidarity and competition. *Eurohealth* 2 4: 19–20.

Hamilton, G.J. (1996) Competition and solidarity in European health care systems. *Eur. J. Health Law* **3**: 323–329.

Harper, P.S. (1993) Insurance and genetic testing. *Lancet* **341**: 224–227.

Jaeger, A.S. (1993) An insurance view on genetic testing. *Forum for Applied Research and Public Policy* 23–25.

Pokorski, R.J. (1995) Genetic information and life insurance. *Nature* **376**: 13–14.

Chapter 2

GENETICS, INSURANCE AND RISK

François Ewald

2.1 INTRODUCTION

The aim of this chapter is to set out how the development of genetics may affect insurance principles and techniques. This question lies at the center of current debates on ethics. It is a very interesting one, because the results that may be reasonably expected of genetic testing remain unclear, and insurance principles and techniques are not widely known. It is therefore appropriate to first deal with several preconceived ideas that may detract from discussions on this issue, which are often highly abstract.

Thereafter, we will consider how insurance principles and techniques may be affected by genetic information. The fundamental notions are those of risk, risk declaration, adverse selection and fairness. Finally, discussion will center on how regulations that have been adopted create the possibility of a compromise between technical insurance requirements and ethical requirements [1].

2.2 THE QUEST FOR KNOWLEDGE

The relation between genetics and insurance is often presented in such a way as to imply that the insurance industry has a particular interest in this new form of knowledge, as if the insurance industry specifically requested genetic information, and even as if it was the driving force behind research. This is seen to be the case because it is felt that the insurance industry is driven by a quest for ever-more information, and more and more information on each policy-holder. The idea is that the insurance industry is determined to get as much information as possible. Even if insurers impose moratoriums, and undertake not to use genetic information, not to ask for tests, and not to request tests as a prerequisite to insurance, these commitments are simply taken to imply a fierce commitment to getting hold of genetic information at a later stage. Two comments should be made here, on the facts and in law.

The fact is that the insurance industry is not the driving force behind the genetic revolution, and that, if it is currently considering this question, it is not so much because it wants this information, but because of the predicted political and social consequences of the developments envisaged in the field of genetics. It is instructive, from this point of view, to consider the reasons for French legislation, in 1994, referring to the need to prevent any possible 'abuses' – even when this hypothetical situation could not yet have occurred. One may also consider the Belgian (1992) and Austrian (1994) laws prohibiting access by insurance companies to genetic information, on principle, at a time when they could hardly yet have been used by the industry. As a matter of fact, laws to this effect, notably in Europe, are preventive laws. They were enacted at a time when genetic issues were not yet of practical concern to insurers. As a matter of fact, they still are not.

What is more, the question of the relation between genetics and insurance is often brought up in a speculative rather than practical way. It is remarkable that, for a long time, discussions have been of a very abstract nature, focusing on the broad principles of law and ethics and calling on unfounded economic models, speculating on the possible consequences of genetic research and its practical applications.

As a result, scientists have justified their research as providing a general explanation of illness based on genetic factors. Human beings will become, thanks to the unfolding of the human genome and genetic mapping, entirely, or almost entirely, transparent. Nature will take the place of nurture. This spells the end of the vision of illness inherited from Pasteur: that of an event caused by aggressive outside agents, against which the organism defends itself. In its place, we are presented with the notion that each of us is the source of our own health, that we are not handed the same deck of cards by nature, and that there is nothing we can do about it. Pasteur's vision was more comfortable: it meant we were not personally responsible, it considered us to be victims of illness, even though, by means of an emphasis on hygiene, it made public health a collective responsibility. The genetic vision makes us responsible for our illness: powerless, but responsible nevertheless, since we are the source of our own illnesses. And even more so in the sense that it makes us responsible for managing our health optimally. Undergoing genetic testing, in such a deterministic context, takes on the aspect of a final judgment, of a bolt from the blue, which we are powerless to change. However, there is no proof that we are condemned to this new determinism. Even researchers themselves no longer share such a simplistic view of reality. Everything seems more complicated today. In fact, it is too early to predict the effect of implementing techniques that would enable us to 'read' the human genome on a large scale. Perhaps a different view – much more complex than those we have adhered to up until now – will come to the fore. We have to be very careful in interpreting genetic information. The genetic revolution is less an established doctrine than a technical measure used to accumulate data, while waiting – almost certainly for some time still – to determine its true significance.

In law, it is important to emphasize that the problem, from the point of view of the insurer, is not to know everything about each of its policyholders, but rather to acquire a minimum of useful information. Although it is true that no insurer can cover a risk without information, the problem, from the insurance point of view, is not to multiply available information, but to use relevant information. It is not a matter of quantity, but of quality. Risk, which is the very nature of insurance, is information. The cost of risk, or, more precisely, of managing risk, varies with the information to be dealt with. In the sense that the risks discussed here are large-scale risks, it is clear that it is in the insurer's interest to deal with as little information as possible. This is why one of the results of genetic information – if it introduces too many variables, thus complicating the analysis of such information – will be to render this information, if not unusable, then at least difficult for the insurer to exploit. Insurers do not currently ask insurance applicants to undergo all medical tests available. It is hard to imagine why it would be any different with genetic testing. Before getting embroiled in overly abstract speculation, it would be useful to consider insurers' actual strategies for obtaining information.

In addition, it should be noted that the insurer is not in command of information on risk. The insurer should also take into consideration the information available to the policyholder, to the extent that this information is likely to determine his/her insurance behavior. This is the practical issue facing the insurance industry. If the insurer is interested in the genetic revolution, it is, first and foremost, because such genetic information, if available to the policyholder, is likely to affect his/her insurance behavior. One may thus distinguish between 'active' information (resulting from the insurer's interest in requesting genetic testing as a prerequisite to offering insurance) and 'passive' information (related to the policyholder's own knowledge of his/her genetic condition) [2]. In no European country have insurers requested that genetic testing be a prerequisite for access to insurance. The only question that has been asked concerns the issue of whether the insurer has the right to ask the policyholder if he/she has undergone genetic testing which has been carried out for a different reason, and whether he/she knows the results.

It is also important to note that the type of genetic information available today is hardly relevant to the insurance industry, except in the case of a few rare monogenic illnesses (such as Huntington's disease). In all other cases, in other words for most common illnesses, currently available genetic information is hardly relevant to life insurance, because it is too uncertain and subject to fluctuations. That is why the British government, while recognizing that genetic information may, in law, concern the insurance industry, has decided that only an independent commission may decide which tests are 'relevant' to insurers.

By the same token, the questions raised on genetics and insurance are often more speculative than practical in nature [3]. There is no pressure on insurers to use genetic testing. However, there is a great deal of pressure, often ideological, on insurers with respect to genetic testing. Some have used this opportunity to try to change certain fundamental insurance principles, such as that relating to risk disclosure or the right to use health-related information to assess risks in the field of life insurance. If insurers have been raising this issue, it is because they have to face often intense lobbying from those who want to use this opportunity to question certain major insurance principles. They seek to contrast insurance law with a sort of 'right to insurance', which, according to them, has become necessary because of the important role of insurance in our daily lives. They consider access to insurance as a prequisite to leading a 'normal' life in society. According to them, this would justify socializing insurance.

Because insurers have not requested genetic information, since such information is still too uncertain, it is understandable that, in several countries, insurers, often backed by public authorities and researchers themselves, have chosen to impose a moratorium. This means that they have decided to wait and see, until genetic research has become a more established scientific field. It is only at this point that the real issues will come to light. It is possible that they will not be those that we imagine today. This is no doubt the reason why the Council of Europe's Convention on Human Rights and Biomedicine, adopted at Oviedo on April 4, 1997, provides in Article 28 that: 'The parties to this convention will ensure that the fundamental questions raised by developments in biology and medicine are discussed openly and publicly, particularly the relevant medical, social, economic, ethical and legal implications, and that their possible applications are discussed by all concerned'.

2.3 THE INSURANCE CONTRACT

2.3.1 Risk and risk transfer

When we refer to insurance, we are talking about private market insurance, in other words a service offered by insurance companies operating in a competitive market. Reference is often made to genetics and insurance in general, but there is no such thing as insurance in general. There are only insurance companies who are in competition with one another [4].

In a competitive market, insurance obeys the laws of supply and demand. The insurer responds to an application for insurance from future policyholders. This concept of applying for insurance is important. While insurance is not obligatory, the insured will apply for insurance on the basis of specific circumstances that give him/her a particular perception of a risk, against which he/she wishes to be insured. Two types of situations can be distinguished. Firstly, the situation may concern an objective assessment of assets that characterize certain periods in the life cycle: providing capital for one's children in the event of death, estate planning, preparing for retirement, securing a loan – all areas in which health reasons hardly enter into the picture or not at all. Another situation is one where the application for insurance is brought about by the discovery that one's state of health, or more precisely, poor state of health, makes obtaining insurance a matter of urgency. In many cases the advantages of obtaining insurance are greater the more threatened one's situation is. It is understandable that, for the policyholder, such a revelation brings home the need for insurance. The insurance applicant wants to obtain insurance, if not because the risk has already occurred, then at least because it seems imminent. This is also what makes insurance so difficult, since the random nature of risk tends to disappear. For the insurer, these two types of behavior are not equivalent. The second, in particular, exposes the insurer to adverse selection. It is clear that if only those individuals who discover a threat to their health applied for insurance, life insurance would no longer be possible. Insurance is linked to two fundamental notions: that of risk, on the one hand, and that of risk transfer by means of a contract, on the other. The insurer commits to accepting an individual's risk by means of a contract.

2.3.2 The concept of risk

Risk is the fundamental notion in insurance, constituting its very nature and purpose. Behind the notion of risk, there is that of random variables. Risk refers to an event that is possible, or more or less probable, but never a certainty. Without it, insurance would not be possible. Risk expresses the probability of a given loss. The premium is a fraction of its value. The notion of risk itself is linked to that of expectancy, such as life expectancy in life insurance. Risk is the current value of a future event, whether this event is joyous or unhappy, desired or feared. What is more, this risk needs to be evaluated. The insurance business involves putting a price on risk. The risk is virtual, it lies in the future, it does not (yet) exist. The insurance business involves putting a price on risk *before the fact*. This evaluation is never certain. It may even be risky. By definition, the information available for the risk is never complete. That is why, in France at least, an insurer cannot be an individual, but must be a legal entity. The insurer may assume risks on behalf of individuals because it has already assumed the risk of other individuals, and these risks will cancel one another out within the group of insureds thus constituted. This is the difference between insurance and betting. While certain risks will occur, others will not. This means that a balance will be reached, enabling the insurer to honor its commitments.

The insurer is able to cover a given risk and put a price on it that equals only a fraction of the possible loss, because it relies on the principle of mutuality and probability, two concepts that are, in fact, closely related. Probability presupposes mutuality; a mortality table gives the average life expectancy of an individual, or of an average individual at a given age, in other words that which corresponds to the risk of each insured, if the entire population were members of a mutual insurance company. It reflects the life expectancy of a particular individual only if this individual corresponds with the average, which is never exactly the case. The statistics linked to the principle of mutuality make it possible to predict the probability of a risk. Mutuality makes it possible to spread the risk. For this reason, the insurer will aim to keep its portfolio homogenous and balanced, at least in terms of rates charged [5].

Insurance is based on the notion of actuarial justice, equity and fairness. This has several implications. Firstly, in terms of the group of insureds, each individual does not present the same level of risk. A mortality table sets out the average life expectancy of individuals in a given population, and not that of each and every individual, which is determined by both known and unknown factors. The notion of actuarial justice involves insuring that each individual's contribution corresponds to his/her risk level. This implies that each individual pays what he/she owes. Neither more nor less. In principle, one individual's contribution should not subsidize that of another. Secondly, actuarial justice includes the notion that individuals who seek membership of an insurance pool have an obligation to be truthful, vis-á-vis the other members. He/she should not withhold information that would be relevant to his/her risk level simply because this information would be to his/her disadvantage. Finally, actuarial justice results from a competitive market; in such a context, a company that does not put a realistic price on risk will soon be ousted by a competitor who can offer policyholders better rates for the same coverage. Competition means that the price the insurer charges for covering a risk tends to be more fair. This benefits the insured, who would otherwise be charged rates that corresponded to his/her fear of risk, rather than the actual risk involved [6].

In addition, the insured wants his/her risk to be rated at a fair price, at the exact price it represents for the group of insureds, neither more nor less. The insured, by definition, does not want to contribute more than he/she owes. If so, he/she will seek out another insurer, or reject insurance altogether [7].

2.3.3 The nature of the insurance contract

A second notion which is central to insurance is the transfer of risk by means of a contract. The insurance contract is irrevocable. The insured has the obligation to describe the risk to be transferred as precisely as possible. For its part, the insurer accepts or does not accept this risk, defines it, and sets boundaries and limits to it (unfortunately known as 'exclusions') and commits to it. Whatever happens to the insured, the insurer is liable. It may not argue that it was unaware of any particular circumstance. It has to take this upon itself. Even more so since it has the right to ask the insured questions regarding the nature of the risk to be covered.

The notion of a contract is what distinguishes private insurance from social insurance. The relation between the insurer and insured in social insurance does not involve a contract, but an 'obligation'. If the social insurer wants to modify premiums, the member has no say in it. The same goes if the insurer wants to change the amount of benefits. This type of adjustment is not possible in private insurance. If it were, insurance would make no sense [8].

Insurance means covering a risk *before the fact*. This is what distinguishes insurance from assistance, which is the spreading of the loss burden *after the fact*. Once a risk has occurred, the option of insurance no longer exists. Even if some people think that is when it would be most useful.

Insurance involves several notions of solidarity. Firstly, it is an instance of solidarity in the sense that taking out insurance, in and of itself, involves a sort of awareness of the importance that belonging to a pool increases individual and collective savings. This is what Edmond About explained thus in the 19th century:

> You know that car wheels, through wear and tear on the road, disperses 20 kilograms of iron each day in the streets of Paris. These 20 kilograms of precious metal are not destroyed, but they are lost. The fact that they being divided into almost infinitesimal particles makes them unusable. Suppose that a patient and ingenuous worker succeeds in gathering all these atoms of iron, and restitutes their cohesion, resistance, and all other useful qualities. He puts them in an iron-mill and is left with an iron lever. Has he not created a capital useful to people? A centime is no more a capital than a strip of iron is a lever. It hardly has any value. You will have trouble finding individuals who care about the loss or gain of one centime, because a single centime has no effect on us. But an

> individual who, through honest means, obtains this single, useless centime from all his fellow citizens will create a capital of 10 million, in other words, a lever large enough to move mountains [9].

Where we are nothing individually, we become everything in solidarity. Taking out insurance is therefore not only an individual duty, in the sense that not taking out insurance 'is an act of culpable egotism and recklessness towards one's family (. . .) taking responsibility for one's future misery'. Or where not being insured 'is, in spite of oneself, playing with fire, with the sea, with hail, with death'. It is even a social responsibility: those who do not take out insurance are a double burden on society because of the assistance they would need if they fall victim to an accident, by trying to save the 'centime' which, together with others, could have created capital useful to all. However, insurance also refers to solidarity in another sense: by establishing risk classes and grouping them around an average, insurance sets up cross-subsidies between individual risks, which cancel one another out in the end. In some cases, such as natural catastrophe insurance, these subsidies may be substantial. They form the basis of group insurance. On principle, insurance does not involve a third form of solidarity, that of assistance *after the fact*. The loss has occurred, and an individual – who, for argument's sake, was not insured – is needy and expects charity. Insurance is not a form of assistance. When we refer to solidarity, which is our response to those who have information about their genetic condition, it is important to determine what type of solidarity this entails.

2.3.4 Disclosure of risk

The preceding notion has several consequences on the way the insurance relationship operates. We will examine those which directly concern the issue of genetics, in other words those that concern the rules governing the disclosure of risk. It is easy to understand that it would be impossible for an insurer to cover a risk that it cannot assess. Risk assessment alone allows the insurer to determine whether the risk can be assumed. Insurance is, above all a *personal* contract. The insurer's responsibility is to honor its commitments. It is responsible for determining which risks it can and cannot accept. In other words, what is insurable. The insurability of a risk is not determined in any general sense, but company by company, according to size and portfolio. This is why the concept of refusal to sell does not, except in unusual circumstances, apply to insurance. The better a risk is identified, the more insurable it is. People sometimes say that the more that is known about a risk, the less insurable it will be. This is totally false. Or, more precisely, this statement confuses risks with claims: information about a risk does not imply any certainty that it will occur, but simply an accurate assessment of its probability. This makes the risk insurable. Anything else is increasingly precise knowledge that the risk has already occurred, or is imminent.

Risk assessment depends on two types of information: statistical information, which provides an average risk measurement or a measurement of average risk, and specific information regarding a particular individual risk. These two types of information complement one another without overlapping. The first type concerns knowledge at the insurer's disposal, the second type that at the insured's disposal. Each of the two parties to the insurance contract has particular types of information regarding the risk at their disposal.

For this reason, we refer to skewed information: the insurer with respect to its policyholders, who are hardly concerned, nor should they be, by the latest mortality tables. And the insured with respect to the insurer, who hardly has the means to know who its policyholders are. The insured alone has information concerning his/her private life, which, for example in health insurance, is specifically protected. The fact that skewed information exists between insurer and insured creates problems for the functioning of the insurance relationship, since it is relevant to the rules governing disclosure of risk. These rules fulfill three main requirements: the first is linked to the notion of a contract, the second to the fact that insurance is offered on a competitive market, and the third to considerations of equity and social fairness.

The insurance relationship takes the form of a contract. The insurance contract should therefore fulfill the major contractual requirements, particularly regarding the validity of consent, which tends to be a particular problem in insurance [10]. Although the insurer personally contracts with each individual insured, the contract as such sets out the insurance terms which structure the mutuality as a whole. This means that the insurance contract is, by nature, a contract in set form. The insured is asked to fit into a predefined framework, namely that structuring the insurance mutuality. The contract is only valid if consent is not vitiated by an 'error' regarding its aim. This is particularly relevant to insurance, because risk, which is the aim of insurance, is virtual and can only be determined in an incomplete way. Rules applicable to risk disclosure aim to ensure that consent is not vitiated, and that there are as few misunderstandings as possible. These obligations concern both the insurer and the insured. The insurer has to provide advice and information on the nature of coverage and, therefore, on the risk for which cover is being offered. However, most obligations in terms of risk disclosure fall to the insured. In principle, the insured should disclose everything likely to impact on the risk for which he/she is seeking coverage. If the risk concerns life expectancy, this means all information available that may impact on it. This could include information regarding his/her state of health. All of this information, by definition, is only available to the insured. In practice, insurance law sets out the rules for this declaration. According to the French Insurance Code, the insurer is responsible for asking specific questions which, from its point of view, are relevant to risk assessment. The insurer cannot complain that the insured replied inaccurately if the questions it asked were too general in nature. However, the insured is under an obligation to reply honestly, without withholding information, for example by citing the confidentiality of medical information [11]. A false statement, if it can be proven, is always punished – by canceling the contract, if the false statement was intentional. Truthfulness in the disclosure of risk is a fundamental principle of insurance law.

These rules are also there for other reasons. The first is that they are a prerequisite to the optimum functioning of the insurance market. The biggest risk for the insurer is the risk of adverse selection. This means that a particular insurance company may find itself attracting 'bad' [12] risks in relation to the rates charged. Its portfolio is unbalanced. It will have more claims than expected, and will be forced to increase its rates. This means that it will lose its 'good' risks, in a vicious circle which will inevitably lead to bankruptcy. Adverse selection results from skewed information between the insurer and the insured. It can only be prevented by the insurer's ability to reestablish a certain level of equality of information with the insured. It is clear that, if a law should prohibit insurers from asking the insured any questions relevant to its seeking an insurance contract, it would certainly expose insurance companies to the risk of adverse selection. The result would be a rise in the price of insurance for the market as a whole, which may make insurance too expensive for 'good' risks The latter may thus reject insurance altogether. This would result in a collective decline in well-being and could perhaps even lead to the withdrawal of the product from the market.

There is another reason for the strict rules concerning the disclosure of risk: preventing fraud and insurance speculation. The fact is that a dishonest proposer who wants to obtain risk coverage at an unrealistic rate, in other words for less than it is worth, knows that this advantage will be paid for by other members of the group of insureds. By way of an excuse, the (rather unpopular) insurer is seen to be bearing the cost that is, in fact, borne by other members. As they say, 'The insurer will pay'. In this game, the wealthiest person obviously gains the most: the wealthier you are, the more it is in your interest to hide what you know about your risk. It is those with less money who have to bear the costs of this unfairly obtained advantage. This is totally contrary to equity and social justice.

2.4 THE CONSEQUENCES OF GENETICS FOR INSURANCE

This issue should be considered from two points of view. The first question concerns whether genetic information is useable by the insurance industry. In what way? The question may seem absurd, as it would appear to be obvious. However, things are often more complicated than they seem. It is also necessary to consider the regulatory consequences that genetic threats have already brought about, and may still bring about, for the insurance industry and its legal framework. They are, in fact, busy changing insurance law and practices profoundly.

2.4.1 Can the insurance industry use genetic information?

Firstly, genetic information describes a risk in the insurance sense of the word [13]. The presence of a particular genetic marker indicates a probability, a deviation from an average likelihood of suffering from a given condition, except in the case of monogenic diseases, which may show a very clear, deterministic correlation between a genetic difference and the disease in question, even if the disease is not currently present. There is a certain epistemological similarity between insurance and genetics. Genetic information does, in fact, constitute the evaluation of a risk. Insurance and genetics are both offspring of the 'probabilistic revolution' [14]. From this point of view, it is difficult to see why genetic information would not be usable by the insurance industry.

However, this is all very theoretical in nature. In any event, because the interpretation of available genetic information still reflects large variations at the present time, it does not clarify long-term commitments of the type made by the insurance industry. The argument is often made that if insurers had this information at their disposal. This would lead them to exclude certain policyholders from insurance. This is an incorrect conclusion. It may be based on a poor understanding of the nature of genetic information. The insurer's role is to insure. Proof of this is that 99% of all applications for insurance are accepted, 4% of them as aggravated risks. And recent events in the insurance industry have shown that insurers continually extend the scope of what is insurable, as in the case of cancer and acquired immune deficiency syndrome (AIDS). Genetic information would only exclude certain policyholders from coverage if it took away the random nature of risk. Generally speaking, though, it will only enable risks to be better assessed; in other words it will position each individual within the group of insureds in a more accurate way. It is quite clear that genetics is not expected to change the laws of mortality. It may only enable us to determine more accurately how it will be distributed in the population. In addition, genetic information could hardly have any effect other than leading to a redistribution within the group of insureds, and not of an exclusion from this group of insureds. What this means, in practical terms, is that a person may move from an average risk category to an aggravated risk category, or vice-versa [15]. Genetic information also concerns the insurance industry in the sense that, if it is available to the insured, it is likely to influence his/her application for insurance, thus reinforcing the problem of adverse selection.

The epistemological similarities between an insurance risk and a genetic risk do not necessarily imply that genetic information should be used by the insurance industry. This would, in fact, depend not only on the reliability of data, but also on the insurance line and the type of risk in question. In principle, genetic information could only be used by insurers if it is reliable, stable, and forms part of established scientific knowledge. This is for several reasons: the insurer should limit the risk of errors, particularly with regard to long-term commitments. Here again, its objective is to put the most accurate price on risk. Price is what defines the quality of its service. Some may contend that it is in the insurer's interest to increase this price as much as possible. This could, however, only be the case if insurance companies were not in competition with one another. In addition, if the insurer were to use unconfirmed information that is subject to variation, it may be accused of using arbitrary data. This could be considered a form of discrimination to be punished, which would have the effect of dissuading insurers from using such information. For both these reasons, the generalized use of genetic testing in insurance is hardly envisaged in the short term.

In addition, it should be noted that genetic information is not relevant to all types of insurance. Here a distinction needs to be made between different types of life insurance, which are, by definition the only types concerned by genetics, depending on the various coverages offered. Health insurance and the various types of life insurance are not the same in this regard. The first type of insurance provides access to health care which, in European countries, is considered a 'necessity'. Life insurance, for its part, involves an individual's estate, his/her personal wealth and assets. So does death insurance, which is the insurance of a capital amount in the event of death. The same goes for credit insurance, which involves coverage of borrowed capital in relation to ownership of a particular asset. It is not clear that these different types of insurance can be dealt with in the same way. In addition, in Europe access to health care is generally covered by social insurance, characterized by the fact that all individuals have unconditional access to it, regardless of their level of risk and wealth. Should we guarantee access to credit insurance in the same way as we guarantee access to health care? And, what is more, should we confuse access to loans with access to insurance for such loans?

Statutory differences in European countries between health insurance and life insurance testify to the fact that they do not involve the same type of assets, even if some individuals maintain that life insurance, at least some forms of life insurance, is sufficiently widespread to constitute a prerequisite for a normal life in society. For this reason, they maintain that life insurance should be accessible to all, in the same way as health insurance [15]. This boils down to arguing for the right to life insurance which – in this case scenario – would be independent of risk. This would mean using insurance to set up cross-subsidies between income, capital and various properties where, as we have already shown, the individual with the most advantages is not necessarily the one with the least money. Institutionalizing such a right would not only make life insurance, but also wealth, income and estates, more social in nature. It would positively discriminate on the basis of risk distribution: it would ensure that individuals with the least favorable genetic make-up are compensated by gaining access to certain assets. Insurance, in this hypothetical case scenario, means accepting, in addition to taxation, the subsidizing of other individuals' estates, which are of a purely personal nature. This would boil down to making life insurance part of public policies to promote wealth and spending. It is easy to imagine the consequences of such a measure: it would result in low-risk individuals rejecting insurance. This would lead to a form of adverse selection (and discrimination) and would deprive that part of the population which refuses to be part of such public policy from insurance.

We have already referred to the risk, which is scientifically highly unlikely, that one day, genetically low-risk individuals would demand preferential rates. The real risk is more likely that the average risk population will reject insurance if general rules regarding the disclosure of risk were to be suspended with respect to genetics. Average risk individuals would consider that this should not be used as a mechanism to stimulate spending.

It may be argued that, in practice, the principle of mutuality already applies to life insurance, to the extent that individualization of risk remains limited. The insurer uses a general mortality table, whereby 95% of risks correspond to the average life expectancy, and only 4% represent excess mortality. Doesn't this type of pooling principle characterize group insurance? Why then not extend this notion of the mutuality principle? Would the cost, spread over all insureds, not be imperceptible? That may be true. However, it should be noted that this insurance pooling is not applied blindly, but results from information about individual and collective risks. Risk classes are constituted with transparency and equality, which makes them acceptable to insureds. This would not be the case if the insurer were unable to assess risks because these were concealed in one big group of insureds. This would transform the nature of insurance. It is not the same thing to extend the mutuality principle to aggravated risks by means of appropriate techniques and to redesign insurance by starting off with the specific problem of aggravated risks, calling the fundamental principle of the disclosure of risk into question.

2.4.2 Conflicting principles

Insurers, at least in Europe, do not use genetic information. They do not make genetic testing a prerequisite to offering insurance, and do not ask to know the results of any tests undergone. Genetics does not form part of current practice. This has not prevented regulatory authorities in several European countries from taking a number of steps to prevent 'abuses', in other words to prevent any use of such information that may be construed as discrimination. This is, in any event, the interpretation one may conclude from both the Council of Europe's Convention and the UN Declaration [16].

Two main approaches can be identified here. The first is that of countries which prohibit the use of genetic information by insurers outright, such as Belgium and Austria. The second approach is that of countries which authorize access to genetic information, but under conditions that significantly change the status of risk assessment in insurance. This is the case in the United Kingdom where an attempt is being made to find a compromise between insurance techniques and regulations regarding discrimination.

It is in the insurers' interest to protect themselves against the consequences of skewed information. This limits access by insurance: it does not provide limitless access to the results of genetic tests, but only enables insurers to avoid the consequences of skewed information, or adverse selection. This results in a wide range of limits on access to genetic information. Therefore, according to the Genetic Code of Practice of the Association of British Insurers [17], one notes that insurers undertake not to request any genetic test as a prerequisite to offering insurance (Art. 2), but reserve the right to ask insurance applicants to disclose any specific knowledge they have of their risks (Art. 3 and 4). Another limit concerns the amount of capital insured (£100 000, according to Art. 27). Insurers are only allowed to ask insurance applicants about any results of genetic testing if the capital amount exceeds a certain limit. It may, in fact, be assumed that the risk of adverse selection only truly comes into play with large capital amounts. This creates a separate group within the group of insureds, and provides that different terms and conditions apply to it [18]. These two rules clearly show the problem: knowledge by the insured of his/her risk in the event of insurance of capital above a certain amount.

In addition to these rules, we find two main principles. British insurers undertake not to charge those who claim to be 'good' risks less (Art. 5 and 33), which boils down to prohibiting insurers from setting up a subgroup to favor such low risk insureds. In addition, British insurers subscribe to the fundamental principle that the result of a genetic test may only be taken into account if it is reliable (in terms of the results obtained) and relevant to the risk insured (Art. 29 and 41). This constitutes a new limit on the use of genetic tests: the notion of reliability means that British insurers are prevented from asking questions regarding the results of genetic tests except perhaps in the case of rare monogenic illnesses such as Huntington's disease. The aim here is to prevent the use of genetic tests if it would constitute arbitrary information. The principle of relevance, together with a requirement that insurers state the reason for their decisions (Art. 7) and the option of an appeal launched by insureds (Art. 20, 39 and 40) aim to establish the principle that the test should be appropriate and proportional to the risk covered. All this aims to ensure that risk assessment does not constitute unfair discrimination.

These proposals have been adopted by the British government, which authorizes insurers to ask an insurance applicant whether he/she has undergone genetic testing, provided that this test is 'relevant' to the insurer, in other words for the risk involved. The relevance of a test will be determined, not by insurers, but by an independent Commission [19]. As we have seen, the problem is to avoid arbitrary information resulting from the use of tests with unconfirmed predictive value, and to ensure that the test is proportional to the risk involved. The result is that the authorization in principle of asking about genetic testing does not mean that the question can actually be asked. It all depends on one's interpretation of what is a relevant test. Firstly, it is clear that this means that the test is reliable, that it will have some predictive value regarding the risk in question, and will not fluctuate over time. This aims to avoid arbitrariness in the choice or interpretation of tests. There should be a correlation between the test and the risk. It also means that the test should be relevant to the risk to be insured, in other words the proportionality of the test to the risk. In this regard, British regulations are similar to those in the Netherlands on medical testing [20]. The notion is that insurers may have access to genetic results, but because of the principle of proportionality, they may only be used on a case by case, type by type, risk by risk and test by test basis.

2.5 CONCLUSION

These provisions, in their totality, from insurers and regulators, indicate that the standard question regarding access, on principle, by the insurance industry in general to genetic tests in general is unanswerable. This is the case because it is impractical, both in terms of genetic information and in terms of problems in the insurance industry. It should be rephrased into a case-by-case evaluation of tests and their relevance to a given risk to be insured. A question regarding the principle becomes a whole range of practical questions, which cannot be answered abstractly, but only on an ad hoc basis. This makes any intervention by legislators particularly inadequate.

NOTES

1. The argument developed here considers the European context, and only applies to life insurance.
2. Cf. François Ewald and Jean-Pierre Moreau (1994) Génétique médicale, confidentialité et assurance. *Risques*, no. 18, April–June, pp. 111 *et seq.*
3. For two examples of such speculation in the French literature see: François Bourguignon and Jean-Jacques Duby (1995) Médecine prédictive, nouvelles inégalités ou nouvelle solidarité. *Risques*, no. 21, January–March, pp. 125 *et seq.* and the *Cahiers du Comité consultatif national d'éthique pour les sciences de la vie et de la santé*, Génétique et médecine: de la prévention à la prévention, no. 6, January 1996, notably the Rapport éthique, pp. 21 *et seq.*
4. The question of genetics can also apply to social insurance, to the extent that it may lead certain individuals to cancel their policies. However, this type of insurance is not dealt with in this chapter.
5. Cf. Joël Winter (1998), 'L'assurance vie'. In: *Encyclopédie de l'Assurance* (eds Ewald F. and Lorenzi J.H.) Editions Economica, Paris, pp. 731 *et seq.*; Pierre Petauton (1996) *Théorie et pratique de l'assurance vie*. Editions Dunod, Paris.
6. Cf. Pierre-André Chiappori (1997) *Risque et assurance*. Editions Flammarion Collection Dominos, Paris, pp. 63 *et seq.*
7. 'L'effet pervers de l'antisélection consiste à faire disparaître des pans entiers de l'activité considérée', *ibid.*, p.78.
8. On the notion of the contract forming the basis of market insurance as opposed to social insurance, cf. Denis Kessler (1995) 'Comment réformer l'Etat-Providence?, Droits sociaux et garanties contractuelles'. *Revue des Sciences Morales et Politiques*. Editions Gauthier-Villars, Paris.
9. Edmond About (1866) *L'Assurance*. Librairie de L. Hachette et Co., Paris, p. 35.
10. Cf. Jean-Antoine Chabannes and Nathalie Gauclin-Eymard (1992) *Le Manuel de l'assurance vie*. Editions de l'Argus, Paris.
11. This places a strict burden of non-disclosure on the insurer.
12. Risk is 'good' or 'bad' only in relation to the rates charged by a given insurance company not a judgment on individual insureds. They are simply relative to the rates of a given insurance company.
13. See for example: *Cahiers du Comité consultatif national d'éthique*, Rapport scientifique, pp. 10 *et seq.*
14. Lorenz Krüger *et al.* (eds) (1987) *The Probabilistic Revolution*, MIT Press. Cambridge, MA.
15. For example in the case where an individual from a family affected by Huntington's disease has a negative test result for this gene.
16. On this question regarding the nature of assets concerned by various types of insurance, see Alex Mauron (1996) Médecine prédictive et destinées individuelles: la tension entre équité actuarielle et justice sociale. *J. Int. Bioéthique*, **7**: 308; Trudo Lemmens (1999) Private parties, public duties? The shifting role of insurance companies in the genetic era. In: *Genetic Information, Acquisition, Access, and Control* (eds A.K. Thompson and R.F. Chadwick), Kluwer Academic, Dordrecht, pp. 31 *et seq.*
17. 'Any form of discrimination against individuals on the basis of their genetic status is prohibited', Art. 11, Chapter 4, Convention on human rights and bioethics; 'No

one shall be subjected to discrimination based on genetic characteristics that is intended to infringe or has the effect of infringing on human rights, fundamental freedoms and human dignity', Art. 6, Universal Declaration on the Human Genome, UN, 1998.

18. *Genetic Testing, ABI Code of Practice*, The Association of British Insurers, December 1997.
19. Which is already the case, and is not the result of genetics.
20. Government Response to the Human Genetics Advisory Commission's Report on The Implications of Genetic Testing for Insurance, November 1998.
21. See M.G.V. Smittenaar (1998) La Nouvelle Réglementation des examens médicaux aux Pays-Bas, *CEA Info*, No. 57, July/August.

Chapter
3

GENETIC DISCRIMINATION

Veikko Launis

3.1 INTRODUCTION

A common line of criticism concerning modern human genetics and its applications is that it provides a new ground for discrimination among individuals, comparable in some important respects to the more traditional forms of human discrimination, notably racism and sexism. The ground the critics are referring to is the still expanding information concerning people's genetic makeup. Although the ground in itself is not totally new (as we know, race and sex are also genetically determined characteristics), many of the ethical issues and concerns it raises certainly are. Among the most serious concerns pointed out by the critics is the fear that, if third parties such as insurance companies and employers are given access to an individual's genetic information, this will inevitably lead to widespread social and economic discrimination of the most objectionable kind. The term customarily used to describe such an unwelcome result is 'genetic discrimination'.

Leaving aside the issues arising from medical confidentiality (to be dealt with elsewhere is this book), the moral cornerstone of the criticism seems to be that it is wrong to use individual genetic information for discriminatory purposes because, from the moral point of view, the losers of nature's genetic lottery do not deserve their bad fortune any more than the winners of the genetic lottery deserve their good fortune. At first glance, the affinity between genetic discrimination and racial discrimination seems striking. As Peter Singer has remarked:

> The person who is denied advantages because of his race is totally unable to alter this particular circumstance of his existence and so may feel with added sharpness that his life is clouded, not merely because he is not being judged as an individual, but because of something over which he has no control at all. (Singer, 1978, p. 195)

Analogously, to discriminate against a person on the basis of genetic information obtained by genetic testing is to disadvantage him or her on the basis of accidental, morally irrelevant characteristics. It is exactly this feature that makes, in Singer's view, racial discrimination 'peculiarly invidious'.

From the viewpoint of third parties, the issue looks of course different. First of all, as the spokespersons of insurance companies have been quick to argue, differentiation based on genetically determined characteristics has been an approved (or tolerated) practice in insurance business for quite a long time [1]. Thus, the familial inheritance of many well-known genetic disorders such as Huntington's disease and cystic fibrosis is already taken into account in determining whether, or on what terms, to offer coverage to individuals (AHC, 1995, p. 329; Jaeger, 1993, p. 25; NCB 1993, p. 70). It is argued that the fact that the same information can now be obtained by genetic testing does not bring anything new to the picture.

Second, and more important, it might be argued that discrimination among persons is, and should be, *intrinsic* to the nature of insurance (cf. Beider, 1987, p. 70; Hall, 1996, pp. 16–17; Kass, 1992, p. 8; Pokorski, 1997, p. 209). The real business of insurance is accurate risk classification and differentiation grounded on the idea that the premiums should be (more or less) in proportion to the estimated risk level of policy holders. As Peter Harper has explained:

> Insurance is based on the complementary principles of solidarity and equity in the face of uncertain risks. Solidarity implies the sharing by the population, as a whole or in broad groups, of the responsibility and the benefits in terms of costs, while equity means that the contribution of an individual should be roughly in line with his or her known level of risk. (Harper, 1993, p. 224)

It is the latter principle, the principle of equity or actuarial fairness, that seeks to justify treating insurance applicants at different risk differently. According to this view, questioning that principle would undermine the basic idea of private health and life insurance (see Murray, 1992).

Similar arguments can be presented in defense of genetic discrimination in employment. Again, we may be asked to recall that, employers have throughout history selected job applicants on the basis of certain hereditary characteristics that are believed to improve job performance and make workers less vulnerable to work-related hazards and illnesses (Suzuki and Knudtson, 1989, pp. 160–161). Against this background, there seems to be little that is new in using predictive genetic testing for such purposes. And as before, it can be maintained that it is an essential and morally legitimate part of employment practice to discriminate among job applicants and employees according to certain risk factors both to minimize economic loss and to protect those who are specially vulnerable to work-related hazards and injuries (Draper, 1991, pp. 153–155; NCB, 1993, p. 56). Arguably, it is as much in the interests of workers as in the interests of company officials to be successful in preventing high-risk individuals from contracting occupational illnesses.

Taken together, these considerations suggest that there is a genuine ethical problem as to whether and, if so, on what conditions certain discriminatory practices based on hereditary differences among individuals can be morally justified. In the present chapter, an attempt is made to consider this problem in more detail by clarifying the concept of discrimination. Although the problem would clearly deserve a thorough discussion both in the context of insurance and in employment, the analysis here will focus exclusively on the former.

Before beginning, it should be noticed that the problem begs a prior (conceptual) issue: Is it, on the whole, possible to speak about discriminatory practices in a value-neutral way? Although discrimination literally means the power or capacity to make fine distinctions, in popular usage it is often used as a synonym for disadvantaging an individual, or a group of individuals, on the basis of morally irrelevant reasons. In this usage, to call a particular act of discrimination unfair or wrongful would be merely to add emphasis to an already value-laden term (cf. Cohen, 1994, p. 392; Goldman, 1979, p. 23; Sadurski, 1985, p. 187; Singer, 1978, p. 202fn; Wasserman, 1998, pp. 805–806). In what follows, we will deviate from this popular usage and use the term in its older, value-neutral (and perhaps more philosophical) sense, as a synonym for differentiation. In this sense, discrimination can be claimed to amount to morally wrongful or impermissible action only when the characteristics on the basis of which it is made are shown to be irrelevant from the moral point of view.

3.2 TYPES OF DISCRIMINATION

The concept of discrimination is ambiguous not only in its evaluative content, but also in its descriptive or empirical content. In colloquial language, the term is often used as if it were a unified concept, allowing a simple and settled answer to the question of what constitutes discriminatory behavior and what kind of reasons or impulses can be found behind it. On closer examination, however, the concept has a variety of meanings. A distinction can be made between the following dimensions: (i) arbitrary vs. nonarbitrary discrimination, (ii) direct vs. indirect discrimination, (iii) discrimination against person vs. discrimination against behavior, and (iv) statistical vs. individualized discrimination.

These dimensions bear relevance to the problem of moral justification of insurance discrimination based on hereditary characteristics and are helpful in identifying the strongest ethical cases for and against that kind of action.

3.2.1 Arbitrary vs. nonarbitrary discrimination

At least two senses can be given to a claim that some act of discrimination is arbitrary. First, it may be understood as a claim that the act in question is based on characteristics (present or not) that are *irrelevant* to the discriminator's purposes. The characteristics may be considered irrelevant either because there is no (known) connection at all between them and the intended outcome of the act, or because the connection, albeit existent, is insignificantly weak (e.g. an extremely small statistical risk to contract a certain genetic condition). This is what may be called the *broad* sense of arbitrariness. An illustrative example of it is the exclusion of Afro-American applicants diagnosed as having sickle cell trait from the US Air Force Academy in the 1970s because of the unproved assumption that even a single copy of the sickle cell gene might reduce the oxygen-carrying capacity of pilots exposed to high altitudes (Suzuki and Knudtson, 1989, pp. 162–163).

Second, the act may be meant to be arbitrary in the sense that it is based on characteristics that are not present. This is the *narrow* sense of arbitrariness. An example of it would be an automobile insurer who classifies a certain group of car-owners (say, those who have a cellular phone in their vehicle but use it only in the hands-free position while driving) as high-risk drivers, although there is no reliable evidence that the risk of being involved in a traffic accident in that group is higher than the average.

Notice that neither sense of arbitrariness questions the legitimacy of the discriminator's purposes. The purposes may contain, or be based on, prejudices or immoral values or morally insignificant differences, but that in itself does not make discrimination arbitrary as long as the discriminator is committed to the formal requirement of treating relevantly similar cases similarly and relevantly different cases differently. To put the same point differently, a sufficient condition for discriminatory treatment to be nonarbitrary in character is that it be based on characteristics that are prudentially relevant and are exemplified by the person being discriminated against. (To be nonarbitrary in character does not of course mean to be morally acceptable; nonarbitrariness is but a necessary condition of moral acceptability.)

In the light of these considerations, the use of genetic test information for actuarial purposes would seem to be in most cases arbitrary for the present. As the Nuffield Council Report on Bioethics remarks:

> Future research may be able to identify combinations of gene variations which contribute to an actuarially significant greater or lesser risk, or to a greater or lesser likelihood of benefiting from certain sorts of treatment; but at present the genetic information by which insurers could calculate the increased risk to a given individual who has certain susceptibility genes is not available. (NCB, 1998, p. 56)

3.2.2 Direct vs. indirect discrimination

The second dimension concerns the directness of discrimination. Roughly speaking, discriminatory action or policy can be termed direct when the characteristics it is based on are taken intentionally and expressly into account, and indirect when this is not the case (Gregory, 1987, pp. 34–35; Wasserstrom, 1985, pp. 12–13). The case of excluding asymptomatic carriers of sickle cell gene from the US Air Force Academy may be used as an example of the former, since the alleged genetic risk factor was taken intentionally and openly into account in the flight school's admission test. However, since not admitting persons because they have sickle cell trait is in practice similar to excluding them for being black (there is a strong correlation between sickle cell trait and race), the case may also be seen as an instance of (arbitrary) indirect discrimination against blacks.

The matter is, however, more complicated than that. To understand properly what the distinction between direct and indirect action amounts to in the present context, the following senses of 'indirectness' should be distinguished.

First, discrimination can be meant to be indirect in the sense that there is a (contingent) noncausal correlation between what is intended and what is merely foreseen or permitted to result. The correlation can vary from insignificantly weak to almost conceptual necessity (as an example of the latter, think of the correlation between discriminating against applicants who are pregnant and discriminating against women). The stronger the correlation, the harder it will be for the discriminator to remain morally irresponsible for the unintended noncausal consequences of his or her conduct [2].

Second, discrimination can be thought to be indirect in the (more familiar) sense that there is a causal connection between what the discriminator intends to make obtain and what he or she merely foresees or expects to result from his or her conduct. To provide an example:

> Persons with AIDS and those perceived to be at risk are, through the effects of the disease itself, in danger of losing the insurance coverage necessary to pay for it. They are, in addition, increasingly in danger of losing their jobs through the perception of employers that they have at least the potential for raising the costs of group health insurance. (Oppenheimer and Padgug, 1986, p. 21).

The possibility that discriminating against patients with human immunodeficiency virus/acquired immune deficiency syndrome (HIV/AIDS) (and those considered to be at risk of contracting HIV/AIDS) in insurance might expand to their being discriminated against in employment – and perhaps also in some other realms of life – is still a serious ethical concern, particularly in countries where employers are legally responsible for arranging health insurance (see Capron, 1993, p. 31). It is clear that a parallel causal route might be detected in the area of genetic discrimination if the insurance industry started to use the results of genetic tests in underwriting [3].

It should be observed that, from the viewpoint of moral evaluation, facts about *actual* indirect causal consequences have no bearing on the moral status of behavior. This is because whether or not the actual (indirect) causal results will be there is a matter of pure chance. As Jonathan Bennett puts it, the only facts about consequences that bear moral relevance are 'ones about what consequences [the behavior] makes probable' (Bennett, 1995, p. 56, emphasis omitted) [4]. Thus, the moral status of an act potentiating indirect genetic discrimination depends ultimately on two factors: (i) how fair such discrimination is considered to be in itself, and (ii) how probable the act makes it up to.

We can now state, as an intuitive *prima facie* ethical principle, that

(1) It is a morally worse thing to discriminate against persons or groups directly than indirectly. The stronger the correlation between what is intended and what is merely foreseen to result from the act, the harder it is to justify indirect discrimination (cf. Quinn, 1989, pp. 334–335, 338, 343–344) [5].

3.2.3 Discrimination against person vs. discrimination against behavior

The third dimension of discrimination concerns the object (or target) of discrimination. We might suggest, as a first approximation, that discrimination is directed at the *behavior* if it is in the person's power to alter or renounce the behavior, and at the *person* if it is beyond the person's power to alter or renounce the behavior (cf. Goodin, 1989, pp. 110–111). But this is surely too vague. It is, for example, not easy to say whether an insurance company's setting of higher premiums for regular smokers or policyholders who are liable to engage in high-risk sexual behavior should be described as discrimination against the behavior or discrimination against the person. To avoid such difficulties, we might sharpen the distinction by adding that discriminating against the behavior can be regarded as discrimination against the person also when the person has the power to alter or renounce the behavior *if* the behavior is an essential element of the person's identity or lifestyle.

With this clarification in mind, we may suggest, as an intuitive *prima facie* ethical principle, that

(2) It is a morally worse thing to discriminate against the person than to discriminate against the behavior (for which the person can be held morally responsible) (cf. Beider, 1987, p. 68; Hill, 1997, p. 16; Maitzen, 1991, pp. 38–40; Murray, 1992, p. 14; Singer, 1978, p. 195).

As regards discrimination based on genetic information, the relevant question is, to what extent a certain high-risk behavior is determined by factors that are under a person's control and are unimportant to his or her identity or lifestyle. It is frequently argued, inspired by genetic essentialism, that information about an individual's genotype is 'indicative of fundamental and immutable characteristics of that individual', whereas characteristics shaped by the environment are 'incidental, under our control, and thus, more easily changed' (Alper and Beckwith, 1998, p. 143; see also NCB, 1998, pp. 2–3). However, such a view drastically oversimplifies the relationship between genes, environment and personal identity. It is anything but clear why the genetic contribution to a certain multifactorial disease such as cancer or coronary heart disease should be considered more essential to an individual's identity than the environmental contribution; and it is plainly not true that the environmental component is always under the individual's control (think, for example, of environmental hazards such as air pollutants and industrial chemicals that can be extremely hard to isolate, let alone eliminate) [6].

3.2.4 Statistical vs. individualized discrimination

Finally, we should distinguish between statistical and individualized discrimination. Discrimination is called statistical when some identifiable personal characteristic A is positively but imperfectly correlated with some other characteristic B and one discriminates among persons on the basis of A (A being used as a proxy for B). Correspondingly, discrimination can be called individualized when one discriminates among persons either directly on the basis of B, or on the basis of A when there is a perfect (positive) correlation between A and B (cf. Maitzen, 1991, p. 23).

A paradigmatic example of statistical discrimination is the automobile insurer who discriminates against young car-owners by charging them higher insurance rates on the basis of statistics indicating that young drivers constitute a high-risk group in traffic. Although the correlation between age and being unsafe as a driver is high, it is clear that not all members of the group are high-risk drivers (some of them may even be low-risk drivers). In this case, there is an imperfect noncausal correlation between characteristics A and B.

Another example of statistical discrimination is the case in which an insurance company discriminates against persons who have taken a genetic test and have a positive test result. There are two variations on this example. In the first version, the genetic test is inaccurate, which weakens the correlation between a positive test result (A) and the presence of the genetic condition (B). In this case, the A-to-B correlation is imperfect and can be either causal or noncausal (depending on the type of the test). In the second version, the genetic test is extremely accurate (sensitive), but there are some other causal factors involved that contribute to the development of the disease. In this case, there is an imperfect causal correlation between A (the presence of the defective gene) and B (the onset of the disease) (cf. CEJA, 1998, p. 16).

An example of individualized discrimination is the case in which an insurance company discriminates against applicants who either have been reliably diagnosed as having a certain dominantly inherited single gene disorder (such as Huntington's disease) or have a genetic disorder whose symptoms are already manifest. In both cases, there is a perfect (one-to-one) causal correlation between A and B. From the point of view of an insurance company, there is a fundamental difference between these two categories (i.e. attempts to predict a disease that has not yet occurred and diagnoses of an already occurred disease), the difference being that one can insure against the risk of contracting a disease even if the likelihood is extremely high, but one cannot insure against the certainty of already having a disease (cf. ABI, 1997, p. 2; Pokorski, 1997, p. 210).

Again, the moral significance of the distinction can be expressed in the form of an intuitive *prima facie* ethical principle:

(3) It is a morally worse thing to discriminate among persons on statistical grounds than on perfectly individualized grounds, and it is a morally worse thing to discriminate against persons on statistical grounds when the correlation between characteristics A and B is noncausal than when it is causal (cf. Beider, 1987, pp. 66–68; Singer, 1978, p. 195).

For some, this principle, expressing merely a relativist moral preference, might seem to be too weakly formulated. It might be objected that the moral badness of statistical discrimination is not a matter of degree but belongs to the category of things that are 'inherently invidious' and 'humanly degrading'. After all, as Peter Singer has remarked,

> To be judged merely as a member of a group when it is one's individual qualities on which the verdict should be given is to be treated as less than the unique individual that we see ourselves as (Singer, 1978, p. 195).

To this, it can be replied, first, that, although there may be cases in which discrimination solely on statistical grounds should be categorically prohibited (consider, for example, the possibility of arresting persons with a 'criminal tendency gene' prior to the commission of any crime), there are also cases in which statistical discrimination can be given what Robert Simon calls a 'pragmatic justification' (see Simon, 1978, p. 37). The idea is that it is often too costly and administratively too difficult to evaluate cases on an individual basis. In a situation like that, if no other relevant information about the candidates is easily obtainable, the correlation is high enough, and the discrimination has a legitimate underlying purpose (i.e. it would be morally defensible as individualized discrimination), then there may be said to be a pragmatic justification for discriminating statistically against all members of the group (cf. Beider, 1987, p. 67; Simon, 1978, pp. 37–40).

Second, it seems obvious – in the light of principle 2 – that the invidiousness of statistical discrimination is a matter of degree and depends at least in part on the nature of the group to which the individual being statistically discriminated against belongs. Presumably, it is (other things equal) more objectionable to discriminate statistically against an individual for being a member of a group that is beyond his or her power to choose to join or separate from (e.g. race or sex) than to discriminate against an individual for being a member of a group that is at least to some extent under his or her power to choose to join or separate from (cf. Beider, 1987, p. 68; Singer, 1978, p. 195).

3.3 A FRAMEWORK FOR THE DEBATE

As a result of the foregoing analysis, we can distinguish between eight ways of discriminating among individuals:

(i) direct statistical discrimination directed at the person;
(ii) indirect statistical discrimination directed at the person;
(iii) direct statistical discrimination directed at the behavior;
(iv) indirect statistical discrimination directed at the behavior;
(v) direct individualized discrimination directed at the person;
(vi) indirect individualized discrimination directed at the person;
(vii) direct individualized discrimination directed at the behavior;
(viii) indirect individualized discrimination directed at the behavior.

Moreover, since each of these ways can be either arbitrary or nonarbitrary in character, we have a total of 16 ways of discriminating among individuals. However, of these, only the nonarbitrary forms are interesting from the moral point of view.

When considering the justifiability of a particular discriminatory action or policy based on genetic characteristics, several factors must be taken into account. First, we must specify the *context* of discrimination. In what sphere of social life does the action or policy occur: in (what kind of) insurance? in (what kind of) employment? in (what kind of) education? (We have already seen that the same action or policy can be considered direct discrimination in one context and indirect discrimination in another.) After having done this, we must take notice of the various *rights* and *interests* of the parties involved in that context. Finally, we must identify the *type* of discrimination and take notice of the *prima facie* ethical principle governing that type.

As so construed, the problem shows its true nature. The real-life examples and future possibilities of genetic discrimination are so varied and so complex that it would be hopeless to suggest a simple normative solution or some kind of categorical imperative that would cover all of them.

NOTES

1. In the words of Robert Pokorski, 'The principle of insurance discrimination was conceded >100 years ago; it operates countless times each day, when insurers charge premiums that reflect the likelihood of a claim' (Pokorski, 1997, p. 209).
2. Of course, there is a natural (psychological) limit to what a person can foresee without intending it to happen. It is assumed here that, at least in normal cases, if a person intends to make A happen, and that *entails* B, then he or she intends to make B happen. But it must be granted, with Jonathan Bennett, that a person may intend A and only foresee B without intending it, even if he or she knows that it is *causally* impossible to have A without B. Whether or not a person intends a particular consequence of his or her act depends, in Bennett's view, upon which of his or her beliefs about the consequences of his or her act *explain* his or her behavior. See Bennett, 1995, pp. 201–203, 209.
3. Underwriting is the process by which risk is assessed and classified for the purpose of determining insurability and setting premiums.

   Examples can be found in which the causal route between what is intended to make obtain and what is merely foreseen to result runs the opposite direction. For example, an employer who refuses to hire applicants with presbyopia discriminates indirectly against the aged. But it is (the process of) aging that causes and explains presbyopia, and not the other way round. For the sake of simplicity, cases of this kind will be ignored.
4. We shall ignore here the difficult question of whether there is such a thing as *moral luck* (i.e. whether luck has any bearing upon the moral status of our acts) and whether it can be ascribed to groups or collectives. For a philosophical discussion on these issues, see Mellema, 1997, pp. 144–152; Nagel, 1979, pp. 24–38; Williams, 1981, pp. 20–39.
5. This principle is, of course, unacceptable to those consequentialists who hold that the moral status of acts depends entirely upon their consequences. But even the full-blooded consequentialist would agree that the principle is intuitively tempting and forms part of what R.M. Hare calls the 'intuitive level of moral thinking' (Hare, 1981, p. 25).

6. As Robert Pokorski writes: 'In actual practice, few of the tens of thousands of applicants underwritten each day with cancer, coronary heart disease, and other chronic illnesses could be categorized as at fault or in control of factors used to predict risk' (Pokorski, 1997, p. 208).

REFERENCES

ABI (Association of British Insurers) (1997) *Genetic Testing: ABI Code of Practice.* Association of British Insurers, London.

AHC (The Ad Hoc Committee on Genetic Testing/Insurance Issues) (1995) Background statement: genetic testing and insurance. *Am. J. Hum. Genet.* **56**: 327–331.

Alper, J.S. and Beckwith, J. (1998) Distinguishing genetic from nongenetic medical tests: some implications for antidiscrimination legislation. *Sci. Eng. Ethics* **4**: 141–150.

Beider, P.C. (1987) Sex discrimination in insurance. *J. Appl. Philos.* **4**: 65–75.

Bennett, J. (1995) *The Act Itself.* Clarendon Press, Oxford.

Capron, A.M. (1993) Hedging their bets. *Hastings Center Report* **23** (May–June): 30–31.

CEJA (The Council on Ethical and Judicial Affairs, American Medical Association) (1998) Multiplex genetic testing. *Hastings Center Report* **28** (July–August): 15–21.

Cohen, S. (1994) Arguing about prejudice and discrimination. *J. Value Inquiry* **28**: 391–400.

Draper, E. (1991) *Risky Business: Genetic Testing and Exclusionary Practices in the Hazardous Workplace.* Cambridge University Press, Cambridge.

Goldman, A.H. (1979) *Justice and Reverse Discrimination.* Princeton University Press, Princeton.

Goodin, R.E. (1989) *No Smoking: The Ethical Issues.* The University of Chicago Press, Chicago and London.

Gregory, J. (1987) *Sex, Race and the Law.* SAGE Publications, London.

Hall, M.A. (1996) Insurer's use of genetic information. *37 Jurimetrics*: 13–22.

Hare, R.M. (1981) *Moral Thinking: Its Levels, Method, and Point.* Clarendon Press, Oxford.

Harper, P.S. (1993) Insurance and genetic testing. *Lancet* **341**: 224–227.

Hill, G. (1997) Justice and natural inequality. *J. Soc. Philos.* **28**: 16–30.

Jaeger, A.S. (1993) An insurance view on genetic testing. *Forum for Applied Research and Public Policy* (Fall): 23–25.

Kass, N.E. (1992) Insurance for the insurers: the use of genetic tests. *Hastings Center Report* **22** (November–December): 6–11.

Maitzen, S. (1991) The ethics of statistical discrimination. *Social Theory and Practice* **17:** 23–45.

Mellema, G. (1997) Moral luck and collectives. *J. Soc. Philos.* **28**: 144–152.

Murray, T.H. (1992) Genetics and the moral mission of health insurance. *Hastings Center Report* **22** (November–December): 12–17.

Nagel, T. (1979) *Mortal Questions.* Cambridge University Press, Cambridge.

NCB (Nuffield Council on Bioethics) (1993) *Genetic Screening: Ethical Issues.* Nuffield Council on Bioethics, London.

NCB (Nuffield Council on Bioethics) (1998) *Mental Disorders and Genetics: The Ethical Context.* Nuffield Council on Bioethics, London.

Oppenheimer, G.M. and Padgug, R.A. (1986) AIDS: the risk to insurers, the threat to equity. *Hastings Center Report* **16**: 18–22.

Pokorski, R.J. (1997) Insurance underwriting in the genetic era. *Am. J. Hum. Genet.* **60**: 205–216.

Quinn, W.S. (1989) Actions, intentions, and consequences: the doctrine of double effect. *Philosophy and Public Affairs* **18**: 334–351.

Sadurski, W. (1985) *Giving Desert Its Due: Social Justice and Legal Theory*. D. Reidel Publishing Company, Dordrecht.

Simon, R.L. (1978) Statistical justifications of discrimination. *Analysis* **38**: 37–42.

Singer, P. (1978) Is racial discrimination arbitrary? *Philosophia* **8**: 185–203.

Suzuki, D. and Knudtson, P. (1989) *Genethics: The Clash between The New Genetics and Human Values*. Harvard University Press, Cambridge, MA.

Wasserman, D. (1998) The concept of discrimination. In: *Encyclopedia of Applied Ethics*, Vol. 1 (ed. R. Chadwick). Academic Press, San Diego, CA, pp. 805–814.

Wasserstrom, R.A. (1985) Racism and sexism. In: *Today's Moral Problems*, 3rd edn. (ed. R.A. Wasserstrom). Macmillan Publishing Company, New York, pp. 1–29.

Williams, B. (1981) *Moral Luck: Philosophical Papers 1973–1980*. Cambridge University Press, Cambridge.

Chapter

4

GENETIC DISCRIMINATION AND INSURANCE IN PRACTICE

Urban Wiesing

4.1 INTRODUCTION

The differentiation practiced by the private insurance industry may well lead to socially undesirable results. The class of people considered to be uninsurable both in health and life insurance will significantly increase as a direct result of risk-rating practices. Other unwanted social effects will also emerge such as restricted access to housing in those systems where mortgages are underpinned by life insurance policies. These problems are not totally novel but have been observed to occur in other well-documented cases, for example, the denial of coverage to those found to be suffering or at risk of HIV infection. For the most part it is precise and actuarially relevant prognostic knowledge that leads to uninsurability. It is important in these cases to distinguish between the moral responsibility of the insurers and the socially undesirable effects. The economically rational behavior of an insurer does not automatically mean that he/she is morally responsible for the socially undesirable consequences of his/her actions. This distinction is particularly significant because any interference with the economically rational behavior of an insurer may lead to problems with commercial viability and therefore – once these difficulties become widespread – with the viability of the private insurance system.

4.2 ISSUES OF MORAL RESPONSIBILITY

There is, however, some evidence that some of the socially undesirable consequences which have been identified are not in actual fact justified according to the economically rational behavior of the insurers. This occurs when the risk rating or differentiation is based on factors which are not in fact actuarially relevant. In this scenario the relationship between the action of the insurer and the moral responsibility for those actions (and their attendant consequences) is significantly different. This is because the rationale which results in the avowedly socially undesirable consequences is not empirically or actuarially justified. The action taken by the insurance company is not therefore justified or necessary. In situations where the actions of the insurer are not economically rational because they are not actuarially justified then the insurance companies have a direct moral responsibility. If they violate that responsibility in a way which leads to socially undesirable consequences then they can be considered culpable.

A further important distinction must be made between a situation where an applicant for an insurance policy perceives that they are being discriminated against and the objective fact that an inappropriately high premium was demanded or an insurance proposal was refused for reasons which cannot be considered actuarially justifiable. Much of the literature of genetic discrimination is based on the reportage of individuals who perceived that they had been the victims of unjustifiable differential treatment based on genotype (Low *et al.*, 1998). Yet clearly not every reported perception of discrimination amounts in fact to actual discrimination. But the literature is partly aware of this problem and provides evidence of genetic discrimination next to the subjective impressions of those who feel they have suffered.

4.3 UNJUSTIFIED DISCRIMINATION

Genetic information can be used according to the rules of insurance, but it can also be used in an unjustified way. It must be accepted that in fact insurance companies will engage in such unjustified behavior to some extent and we must also face the possibility that this unjustified discrimination may occur more frequently as the quantity of genetic information increases. On close scrutiny this phenomenon should not be considered surprising. Instances of unjustified or unfair discrimination are widely reported not only by life and health insurance companies or health-care providers, but also by 'blood banks, adoption agencies, the military, and schools' [1]. In all these situations cases of unjustified discrimination, discrimination against the rational rules of the business have been reported. The consequences of these practices should and could be avoided.

4.4 GENETIC DISCRIMINATION AND INSURANCE: DIFFERENT OPTIONS

There are five different situations in which possible unjustified discrimination based on genotype can occur.

First, carriers of a certain gene may have their proposal for an insurance policy refused despite the fact that the prognosis of their health is not affected in any relevant way. Alternately they may be offered a contract with a higher premium based on the perceived, rather than actual, risk that they bring to the fund.

Secondly, a situation can arise where even though the particular applicant has a higher risk than an average healthy applicant, the increased premium charged to the particular is higher than the actual increase of the risk. Insurers in this situation are demanding a disproportionately high premium or they may refuse to accept a proposal even though a policy with a higher premium would be adequate to offset the increased risk. Thirdly, relatives may have their application for insurance refused despite the fact that they are known to be genetically 'normal' or they may be offered a contract with higher premium only [2]. Fourthly, the same situation can arise where the relatives are asymptomatic carriers of a certain gene. A fifth possibility is that relatives are only permitted to purchase an insurance policy where the increase of the premium is higher than the increased risk. Once again in this situation the insurers may demand disproportionately high premiums or refuse to offer a policy even though a contract with a higher premium would compensate for the increased risk which has been brought to the fund.

In effect this means that we have to face the fact that contracts with disproportionately high premiums or inadequate uninsurability may well result from the increase in genetic information. An atmosphere of genetic scrutiny might lead to discrimination that is not justified by the genetic facts, the prognosis in the individual case and the solidarity interests of private insurers. This kind of discrimination is, according to the classic rules of insurance, absolutely superfluous. Genetic information might become a kind of myth that leads not only to unwanted effects but even unjustified unwanted effects [3].

The number of cases where coverage is unjustifiably denied may be low because insurers want to sell their products, therefore it is not in their economic interests to deny insurance coverage to proposers. On the other hand the incidence of charging disproportionately high premiums is not necessarily restricted by the economic interests of the insurer. The charging of disproportionately high premiums may only be restricted by the market or by agreement among the insurance companies themselves. The outright denial of an insurance contract is usually an event which is not readily accepted by a consumer and is one which is likely to generate a degree of public protest particularly when the denial of the proposal is unjustified on actuarial grounds. On the other hand a case where a disproportionately high premium has been charged will not necessarily be quite so visible as in many cases the consumer may not be aware that he was treated unfairly. In most cases it is impossible for the average consumer to estimate whether a particular premium is disproportionately high.

These unjustified and unwanted consequences arise largely because of a lack of understanding or lack of expertise in relation to the implications of genetic information on the part of the insurance industry. A study from the UK suggests that 'error on the part of insurers rather than a coherent industry wide policy' (Low *et al.*, 1998) is responsible for the unjustified discrimination. Despite the fact that the insurance industry is in theory based on rational knowledge, irrational reactions cannot be completely excluded. As long as insurance operates as a business controlled by human beings, it is unrealistic to expect that every action in a private insurance company will be guided solely by the rational rules of private insurance [4]. For example, not every insurance broker may be informed correctly about the implication of a certain genetic status for insurance; consequently not every broker will be able to apply his knowledge adequately. Sometimes the genetic information is difficult to interpret and apply to a contract. The individual actuary must be able to make fine judgments on the basis of this inadequate information. The responses of actuaries to these limitations may be adequate or not. Even the well informed members of an insurance company may not react adequately and may proceed with unjustified caution.

Paradoxically the 'confusion and ignorance in interpreting genetic information' (Low *et al.*, 1998, p. 1635) may also lead to another effect. Alongside the possibility of unjustifiable discrimination lies that of unjustifiable preference. This will arise in situations where the reaction of the insurers to the new genetic information actually operates in the favor of the applicant. In other words the inappropriate behavior of insurers may lead to both unwanted social effects and to wanted social effects [5]. Most probably, however, the inadequate reaction to the new information in favor of the patient will be a short-term phenomenon because these reactions will operate to the detriment of the insurers. When this becomes evident the policy of the industry will inevitably be changed quite rapidly.

NOTES

1. Geller *et al.* (1996); their conclusion: 'The increasing development and utilization of genetic tests will likely result in increased genetic discrimination in the absence of contravening measures.' (p. 72).
2. There is empirical evidence that even 'people belonging to support groups for families with genetic disorders were not treated consistently by insurers' (Low *et al.*, 1998, p. 1634).
3. Lapham *et al.* (1996) reported about the perception of discrimination among members of genetic support groups: '25 percent of the respondents or affected family members believed they were refused life insurance, 22 percent believed they were refused health insurance, and 13 percent believed they were denied or let go from a job.' (p. 621).
4. This is not limited to the use of genetic information. Allen and Ostrer (1993) reported from their inquiry among directors of life-insurance companies that 'one

medical director told us that prior to his arrival his company denied coverage to individuals less than four feet tall, on the mistaken belief that very short individuals have decreased life spans.' (p. 17).

5. In the case of alpha-1-antitrypsin deficiency the insurers 'are not generally aware of the deficiency and its implications' (Wulfsberg *et al.*, 1994, p. 217).

REFERENCES

Allen, W. and Ostrer, H. (1993) Anticipating unfair uses of genetic information. *Am. J. Hum. Genet.* **53**: 16–21.

Geller, L.N., Alper, J.S., Billings, P.R., Barash, C.I., Beckwith, J. and Natowicz, M.R. (1996) Individual, family, and societal dimension of genetic discrimination: a case study analysis. *Sci. Eng. Ethics* **2**: 71–88.

Lapham, E.V., Kozma, C. and Weiss, J.O. (1996) Genetic discrimination: perspectives of consumers. *Science* **274**: 621–624.

Low, L., King, S. and Wilkie, T. (1998) Genetic discrimination in life insurance: empirical evidence from a cross sectional survey of genetic support groups in the United Kingdom. *BMJ* **317**: 1632–1635.

Wulfsberg, E.A., Hoffmann, D.E. and Cohen, M.M. (1994) Alpha-1-antitrypsin deficiency: impact of genetic discovery on medicine and society. *JAMA* **271**: 217–222.

Chapter

5

SOCIAL AND PRIVATE SYSTEMS OF HEALTH INSURANCE

Urban Wiesing

5.1 INTRODUCTION

The task of this chapter is to systematize the possible relationships that exist between private and social health-care insurance and the potential unwanted social results when molecular-genetic knowledge with significant prognostic value becomes more readily available.

5.2 LIFE INSURANCE

In addition to the problems of health insurance some consideration must be given to the question of life insurance. The issues are rather different, because there is no socialized system of life insurance in existence anywhere in the world. This sector of insurance is totally privatized. Nevertheless it must be mentioned that the social value of life insurance depends on the broader context surrounding its use and on the nature of the social goods that can usually be obtained only with life insurance. The most prominent example is the mortgage for a house purchase which in many countries will be given only in connection with life insurance. In considering the impact of genetic information on life insurance it is necessary to look not only at the number but also at the social status of the people who will be restricted from buying a house if precise prognostic knowledge makes them uninsurable. This information will not necessarily impinge on the wealthy people who can afford a house anyway but rather will cause hardship to people in lower income brackets who will be restricted from purchasing private housing. These are the people who have or will have to cope with the hardships caused by genetic disease.

5.3 SOCIAL HEALTH INSURANCE

The problems arising in health insurance are closely related to the social health-care system in a given society. These systems are always the products of long-term historical developments and are therefore more or less arbitrary. Consequently the crucial decisions about how to shape a social health-care system have usually been made long before the question of new molecular genetic knowledge was on the agenda. The circumstances which pertained at the creation of the social health-care systems were quite different from those which are currently faced in the age of molecular biology. Therefore the undesired social consequences can also be understood as a result of conflicts between old structures and new information.

In a situation where every citizen of a society is a mandatory member of a social health insurance no problems of genetic discrimination or uninsurability arise in relation to genetic knowledge. This is largely the case for example in the United Kingdom. The undesired social consequence that some people will refrain from taking a genetic test or will avoid genetic diagnostic measures because of possible negative effects for future health insurance does not arise. The social insurance system for health care is only interested in genetic information for prevention but not for exclusion of new members as long as it is not possible to exclude new members or to charge a higher premium from members at risk.

In a scenario where the mandatory social health insurance systems cover only a 'decent minimum' standard of health care and additional requirements or needs must be met through private insurance then the possibility of obtaining this extra coverage could be jeopardized for people with 'bad' genes. In this case the uninsurability would be a partial one: only for the additional extra premium above that which is covered by the social system.

If only a small minority of the population is privately insured for health and the pressure is high for the private insurer to behave in a similar manner to the social insurance system it might be possible that the private insurer will indeed behave like that, which is the case for example in Germany. Ten per cent of the German population is privately insured for health. The private insurers are not bound by law to operate in the same way as the social health insurers but do so under a system of self-regulation. The private health insurers do not ask for genetic testing after a contract has been signed. When adults apply for private health insurance, for example 'Beamte' (officials or public servants), the companies do not require a physical examination but only require the completion of an application questionnaire regarding the current health status of the proposer. The companies offer contracts for groups (for example for physicians and for officials) and bind themselves not to reject any applicant from these groups; the premium for adult applicants with illnesses is not higher than 200% of the normal premium.

One result of this method of regulation is that the private insurer cannot offer very attractive policies for people with 'good' genes but will be able to offer contracts to that section of the population without requesting a genetic test. One approach could be to insure all newborn children of parents who are privately insured regardless of their health status. This occurs, for example, in Germany where private health insurance companies do not ask for any information about the health status of a newborn if the parents of the newborn have been insured for a period longer than three months and if the parents apply for health insurance for their baby during the first two months after birth. This would be an effective solution to prevent uninsurability as long as the patients do not change their private health insurance during their life time.

5.4 MIXED INSURANCE SYSTEMS

Different considerations arise in the case of a mixed system where private insurance companies do not operate according to social insurance principles. In such cases a different phenomenon can be observed. The 'bad' genetic risks will be covered by the social system and the 'good' risks by the private system – the burdens are socialized and the benefits are privatized. This means, in effect, that the private insurance sector will become cheap and attractive to those with 'good risks', and the social sector will become more and more unaffordable. In the long run the social system will become too expensive for its members or for the state and the taxpayer to sustain and the financial advantages of private insurance will grow. Such challenges to the social system are likely to emerge in the longer term if relevant genetic or other prognostic information becomes widely available and is used by the private insurers. In such a scenario the balance between the social and private systems could only be maintained if the state interferes with regulation or alternatively if the insurance industry adopts a model of self-regulation. Theoretically the insurance industry can benefit from either of two options. They can either operate profitably using a system of detailed selection of genetic risks or, if they can forge industry-wide agreement, they can operate profitably without detailed selection of the genetic risk.

5.5 PRIVATE INSURANCE SYSTEMS

In countries without any social health insurance system a balance between both social and private insurance sectors is unlikely to occur. In these countries the number of uninsurable people and the number of applicants who can be offered coverage only with expensive premiums will probably be highest. Furthermore, in these countries the tolerance for disclosure of unwanted results from genetic tests is also likely to be high because the people are accustomed to the phenomenon of uninsurability. The social effects of such a situation cannot be estimated only by reference to the number of uninsurable people. Equally important is an analysis of the social status of those who will become uninsurable. The impact will be felt most keenly among those who are already suffering a degree of misfortune. Once again, the additional burdens will be imposed on those who are already struggling or will be struggling to cope with the additional hardships caused by genetic disease. It is not only the number of uninsurable people that is significant but also their fate which should be considered when looking at the social impact of genetic testing.

In all the situations which have been outlined in relation to the problem of genetic information and health insurance one thing is clear. The degree of unwanted social consequences largely depends on the given social health-care system. Here once again we can see that stable and efficient working social systems of health insurance have many advantages in the age of genetic testing.

Chapter

6

GENETIC TESTING AND THE INSURANCE INDUSTRY

Tony McGleenan

6.1 INTRODUCTION

The use of genetic tests as the first stage in the development of predictive medicine clearly raises implications for the insurance and assurance industries. The historical development of insurance has been built on the interplay between the concepts of risk and uncertainty. Where there is a clear risk, and uncertainty about the outcome, and where individuals have enough knowledge and disposable income to try to mitigate the negative outcome of that risk then the conditions for an insurance contract will exist. When a sufficient number of individuals are exposed to a risk such that they can determine the collective benefits of pooling their resources in order to mitigate the effects of that risk then the conditions for a private insurance industry will exist. Predictive genetic testing may alter this classical picture somewhat in relation to the areas of life and health insurance. The attraction for the insurance industry of using genetic technology in this way is not difficult to see. Genetic technology offers the possibility of sophisticated predictive diagnosis. The insurance industry depends on the use of medical information to make actuarial calculations of longevity. Genetic tests appear to offer a simple and cost-effective means of generating the information needed to accurately calculate the risk an individual brings to an insurance fund.

6.2 GENERAL PRINCIPLES OF UNDERWRITING

Actuarial principles developed over the centuries provide a normative framework for the practice of underwriting. These principles have been developed primarily in response to the risks presented in the volatile mercantile and marine insurance worlds. Despite their origins these principles are still applied in all areas of modern insurance. As Ostrer points out:

> Insurance is an economic device for reducing and eliminating risk through the process of combining a sufficient number of homogenous exposures into a group in order to make the losses predictable for the group as a whole (Ostrer *et al.*, 1993).

Underwriting is a practice which has developed over the centuries in order to facilitate the sharing of risk and mitigation of loss through the use of insurance. The practice of modern underwriting can be dated to 1680 when a group of businessmen gathered in Lloyd's Coffee House in London to seek cover for shipping interests. The term underwriting comes from the practice of those who accepted the risk writing their names under the insurance contract (Leigh, 1990). Underwriting only forms one part of the practice of insurance and the best means of evaluating its importance is to consider the general practice of insurance in the round. Barr (1993) argues that five conditions must exist before private insurance along actuarial lines can be considered feasible. These conditions are as follows.

(i) The risk that any one individual claims must be independent of the risk that any other individual claims.
(ii) The insured event must not be certain to occur, or in the case of life assurance, there must be uncertainty about the date of the insured event.
(iii) The probability of a claim must be known or at least estimable.
(iv) The purchaser must not be able to conceal relevant information from the insurer.
(v) The purchaser must not be able to manipulate the probability of claiming (Barr, 1993; MacDonald, 1997).

The practice of underwriting focuses around the third and fourth points. The actuary or underwriter is concerned primarily with determining the probability of a claim (or the extent of the risk brought to the mutual fund by the proposer) and with ensuring that there is symmetry of information between the proposer and the insurer. Where there is asymmetry of information the pure actuarial model of insurance is disrupted and the possibility of adverse selection arises.

In the case of life insurance, which is arguably the more pressing issue in relation to genetic testing in Europe, at least in the short term, the actuary has a number of tools at his or her disposal. Since the insured event is a certainty (death) in these cases the crucial information in the relationship between the proposer and the insured is medical information. There are three primary methods by which the underwriter can obtain this information:

(i) through questions on the proposal form;
(ii) through a report from the applicant's doctor;
(iii) through the results of a medical examination which the applicant takes.

Because of the costs involved underwriting would not be a commercially viable enterprise if all three of these methods were used in all cases. Consequently, the vast majority of proposers are processed using only the first method of underwriting. Where the proposer has a history of ill health or where the sum assured is unusually large the second and third methods are implemented. Insurance companies operate a system of 'medical limits' to determine which of the underwriting methods will be used in a particular case. This method of underwriting illustrates that even before the possibility arose of using genetic information, underwriters and insurance companies have long made it their practice to stratify the risk posed by proposers for insurers according to the risk the individual brings to the insurance fund. Consequently it can be seen that the practice of using medical information in the determination of insurance premiums is by no means a new one.

6.3 RISK RATING IN LIFE INSURANCE

The life insurance industry became possible in 1693 when Edmund Halley, more famous for his astrological discoveries, drew up and published the first mortality tables (Bernstein, 1998). Wilkie (1997) points out that initially life insurance was offered at a single flat-rate premium to all proposers, such a practice being based on the *prima facie* plausible claim that all proposers had a more or less equal risk of experiencing death. As the industry developed it was observed by some within the insurance market that, in fact, not all proposers had an equal risk of death. Indeed, it was possible to construct statistically valid and actuarially significant tables which could predict the probability of death for particular groups. When such tables were constructed it became apparent that statistically significant differences in the likelihood of mortality existed as between males and females. Consequently the life insurance industry began to differentiate between male and female proposers for insurance on the ground that they brought different levels of risk to the insurance fund and should therefore pay differential premiums. Three areas in which the fundamental principles of risk rating in life insurance have been brought to public attention are those of tobacco smoking, HIV infection and the mortgage interest tax relief scheme (MIRAS).

6.3.1 Smoking and life insurance

In 1950 Doll and Hill published their now famous study speculating about the linkage between smoking and lung cancer. As Hennekens (1998) points out Doll and Hill judged smoking to be a cause of lung cancer in the 1950s long before there was any clear evidence of the carcinogenic and mutational effects of tobacco smoke on human DNA. At the time this research was quickly accepted by the medical profession and by actuaries, but it was not until the 1980s that insurance companies felt able to begin differentiating between smokers and nonsmokers in determining the relative risk rating for life insurance. The information on smoking was actuarially relevant from a much earlier stage, but it is instructive to see that the insurance companies felt that up until the 1980s society would not be prepared to tolerate differentiation within a risk-rated insurance market based upon smoking. Pokorski (1997) alleges that misrepresentation of tobacco use is a major example of antiselection in the American life insurance market. In the United States life insurance companies issue significant discounts to nonsmokers. These are defined as those who have not used tobacco products in the last 12 months. Urine specimens are sought to determine the presence of nicotine or by-products. In a study carried out by the Berkshire Life Insurance Company of 32 000 applicants who said they did not smoke or use nicotine products 6% tested positive for nicotine.

6.3.2 Life insurance and the HIV experience

A comparison between HIV testing and genetic testing can be instructive because of the many similarities between the two practices. HIV testing shares many features of the majority of available genetic tests. HIV testing is predictive, it has a variable, but often lengthy, latency period, there is currently no available effective cure and in many instances the disease is fatal (Roscam-Abbing, 1991). In cases where the individual has been affected through a blood transfusion, for example, the HIV infection is, like most genetic diseases, entirely outside the individual's control. Furthermore, in both HIV and genetic testing fundamental human rights to such things as privacy and nondiscrimination may be challenged and abrogated as a consequence of the test results. Both types of test also have in common potentially significant repercussions for insurance. The history of HIV testing and insurance is instructive for the discussion of the appropriate response to the new challenges of genetic testing. The outbreak of HIV on a large scale and the possibility of predictive testing led both to adverse selection by applicants and unjustifiable discrimination by insurers (Bartrum, 1993). Adverse selection was facilitated by the latency period of HIV as individuals could remain asymptomatic for an average period of four years. The insurance company responses were on occasion simply discriminatory. Schatz (1987) for example, reports how one insurance company refused to extend cover to single men involved in employment sectors which did not involve physical exertion [1].

6.3.3 Risk rating and the MIRAS experience

One classic example of adverse selection affecting the life insurance industry came with the MIRAS crisis in the United Kingdom in the mid-1980s. When the Conservative government proposed the introduction of tax relief on mortgage interest in order to boost the amount of home ownership the insurance industry and building societies embarked on a large-scale marketing plan to encourage the sale of endowment assurance mortgages to new home owners and also to encourage those who had existing repayment mortgages to switch to an endowment policy. As a high volume of business was expected in order to expedite the process life insurance companies introduced special shortened proposal forms which contained no medical questions. As Leigh points out this strategy was based on a belief that only reasonably healthy people would actually undertake the purchase of a home and therefore the health profile of the mortgagees would be better than average.

The flaw in the system was that insurance sales agents had personal financial incentives to encourage individuals who had previously been rejected by insurance companies on grounds of poor health to take advantage of the new nonselective system. In the first year of the system the actual number of deaths exceeded the number expected according to the mortality tables by a factor of 50%. In the following years as remedial steps were introduced the numbers fell to 11% and then to 2% (Leigh, 1990). Nevertheless the MIRAS crisis provides one of the more empirically credible instances of actual adverse selection.

6.4 RISK RATING AND HEALTH INSURANCE

Most European countries operate systems of health insurance based on social contractarian notions of solidarity. Health insurance is organized on a society-wide basis and funded either through taxation or through dedicated schemes of national insurance. The underlying rationale for such a structure is the Rawlsian notion that individuals cannot know the likelihood of their succumbing to illness and requiring health-care expenditure. Consequently, since all individuals are under this health-care veil of ignorance, all should contribute equally to a societal fund which will cover the costs of all those who require healthcare. As Light describes it:

> Health insurance (or more accurately, sickness insurance) began as a communal, humanitarian act among members of guilds, or unions or fraternal societies to help each other out when one among them faced disaster through illness or accident (Light, 1991).

This system has functioned (albeit with constantly rising costs) throughout most of Europe since the end of the 1939–45 war. The reason for the success of this system and its widespread popularity among citizens of culturally diverse nations is that it does not differentiate or discriminate between those who pose different levels of risk to the insurance fund. It is not the case, however, that it is impossible to introduce concepts of mutuality and differentiation into health care insurance. Actuarially, such a practice can, and in the United States does, occur. Modern medical technology, particularly predictive medicine, facilitates the rating of individual health insurance proposers according to risk. Such a practice can be carried out using the underwriting methods routinely employed in life insurance. A proposer can be asked to fill out a disclosure form, can be asked to submit details from their general practitioner or can be asked to undertake a medical examination. A great deal can be discerned from all of these sources. Family history can be a good indicator of individual risk where there is a history of hypertension, coronary heart disease or familial breast cancer. Similarly, general practitioner notes and records may contain significant details on the results of cholesterol testing or urine analysis. A full medical examination can utilize all the techniques of predictive medicine in an attempt to discern an individual's risk of disease. It is at this juncture that the power of genetic testing as a diagnostic tool in predictive medicine becomes obvious. Particularly in the case of single gene (monogenic) disorders. In these cases a genetic test can predict with a reasonable degree of accuracy a relatively narrow time frame within which a particular individual will begin to manifest symptoms. The situation with multifactorial disorders, which are by far the larger proportion of 'genetic' diseases, is much less clear cut. Predictions can be made, but given the interaction between environment and genotype necessary to produce the disease state, the accuracy of such tests is reduced and the predictive time frame is expanded. Nevertheless, the technology, particularly genetic technology, exists which can facilitate the introduction of risk rating in health insurance. An obvious question is whether such a practice should be adopted. Should health insurance be subjected to the same type of risk rating as life insurance? The experience of the United States is instructive in assessing the merits of such a course of action.

6.4.1 Health insurance in the United States

Initially, health insurance in the United States developed along a model based on communality and solidarity with the provision of health care being paid for by nonprofit health maintenance organizations (HMOs) such as Blue Cross and Blue Shield (Padgug, 1991; Rothman, 1991). The ethos of Blue Cross organizations was the provision of nonprofit community-based insurance funded by flat-rate premiums. The system began to be eroded in the 1940s when employers and trade unions argued that their able-bodied and healthy employees should be entitled to a lower premium for health insurance. These organizations began to seek these lower premiums outside the community-rated system and private for-profit health insurance developed to meet this demand. This libertarian shift away from solidarity-based systems to those modeled on risk-rated mutuality continues to the present day. In modern times the health insurance market is populated by commercial health insurance organizations, for-profit HMOs and the federally funded Medicare and Medicaid systems. Despite this apparently comprehensive provision American health care is in a state of crisis. Two statistics illustrate the nature of the problem. First, expenditure on health care in the United States is projected to reach $1.6 trillion by the year 2000, a figure which will represent 16.4% of gross domestic product. Secondly, in 1990 the Bureau of Census recorded that 33.6 million people in the United States were without any form of private or state-funded health insurance. This figure represents 13.6% of the United States population and is likely to have increased substantially in the intervening period. In the United States private health insurance pays for roughly one-third of health care provision (Loue, 1993). The majority of these insurance schemes operate on a risk-rated basis.

6.4.2 The economic arguments

The growth of risk rating in health insurance has been premised on a belief that it makes economic sense for large organizations to shave what they can from their insurance premiums through sophisticated underwriting. Light (1991) argues that this argument is significantly flawed for three reasons. First, he contends that competitive risk rating can actually be more expensive in the medium term than group or community rating. This is because the employer/purchaser is assuming that his group of employees has a below-average risk rating. This may not, in fact, be the case as at least half of those who purchase insurance will, by definition, have an above-average risk profile. In addition, the extra administrative costs which are built into the design of ever more sophisticated risk rating policies, the cost of predictive testing and the cost of vetting a workforce to ensure a below-average risk profile all combine to make this a more expensive procedure than simply paying community-rated premiums in the first place. Secondly, Light points out that private risk-rated corporate health insurance actually serves to drive the cost of health care upwards. This occurs because the collective bargaining and cost containment practices which are a feature of health-care systems funded through solidarity-based insurance are absent in a system such as that which exists in the United States. Instead of one major purchaser of health-care services there are a myriad of small insurance companies each seeking different deals with health-care providers. The economies of scale seen in, for example, European health-care purchasing simply are not as prevalent. Thirdly, Light argues, the pernicious effects of risk-rated health insurance cause broader structural economic damage by placing strong disincentives in the way of employers who might ordinarily wish to hire the most competent person for the particular job. It also imposes extra administrative burdens on businesses and places the onus of providing for the uninsurable back on the state and ultimately the taxpayer. Risk rating in health care seems to lead to a form of false economy, the ultimate cost in such a system is significantly higher and provides a significantly poorer service than a community-based system.

6.4.3 The justice arguments

Aside from the economic arguments risk rating in health insurance also raises questions of justice at a number of levels. Light's analysis is that this system actually tends to be unjust even to those who are accepted as commercially viable risks. He bases his argument on the 1988 United States Office of Technology Assessment Report which revealed how, in order to maintain a competitive edge, insurance companies were adopting a variety of strategies to avoid providing coverage for those who are actually insured. These strategies range from charging higher premiums through to punitive exclusion clauses. A study by Mortenson claimed that of those individuals who were forced to pay for their own health care in the United States, 46.8% actually had health-care insurance (Mortenson, 1989). A further disturbing injustice which emerges from this portrait of a risk-rated private health insurance industry is the fact that many of the underwriting decisions used to classify and differentiate according to risk may not in fact be statistically accurate or actuarially relevant.

Whereas much of the debate in Europe has focused on the interrelationship between genetic information and life insurance, in the United States it is the area of private health insurance and genetics which causes most concern. A large quantity of legislation, both at federal and state level has been introduced in an attempt to restrict the use of genetic information by health insurance companies. At the federal level the Health Coverage Availability and Affordability Act makes it unlawful for insurance companies to use genetic information either in the form of test results or familial information to exclude individuals from group health insurance plans [2]. At the state level more than 18 legislatures have enacted laws curbing the use of genetic information. In New Jersey genetic privacy legislation prohibits the use of any genetic information for any insurance or employment purpose without written consent. The Genetic Privacy Act establishes individual property rights in genetic information and uses the notion of informed consent as a control mechanism for the information. Genetic information cannot be collected, retained or controlled without the written consent of the individual. Despite the fact that the legislation is described as 'one of the most comprehensive laws protecting genetic information' in the United States (Charatan, 1996) it does tolerate the use of genetic test results in life insurance and insofar as it only bans 'unfair discrimination' it would also appear to permit certain types of discrimination in the area of life and disability insurance.

6.5 RISK CLASSIFICATION

Once the risk information has been acquired on a particular proposal for insurance the underwriting decision must then be made. Leigh (1990) outlines seven possible classifications which can be recommended by the underwriter. Firstly, the proposal may be accepted at standard rates. In the United Kingdom this is described as the ordinary rates (OR) class. A second possibility is to accept the proposal with an increased premium throughout the term of the policy. A variation on this is to accept the proposal with an increased premium for a limited term of the policy. A fourth strategy is to accept the insurance proposal but with a debt or lien on the sum assured. A fifth is to accept the policy with an exclusion clause, excluding cover in the event of certain illnesses for example. Alternately the proposal can be deferred for a certain period of time or it can be declined outright. In the United Kingdom the percentage of proposers falling into the OR class can be as high as 97% (Leigh, 1990) although the Association of British Insurers (ABI) has recently put the figure at 95% (ABI, 1997a). In Europe the OR rate stands at about 95% (Chuffart, 1996) of all proposals, and in the United States the figure is 91% (Pokorski, 1996) [3]. Broadly speaking in the United Kingdom a ratio of 95:4:1 can be found in life insurance in terms of OR:increased premiums:outright refusals. The figure consistently given by the insurance industry for outright rejections of proposals, both to independent bodies and in their own literature is 1%.

6.6 THE CONCEPT OF ACTUARIAL FAIRNESS

Risk rating is further complicated by the fact that insurance companies operate health insurance on the basis of a concept of 'actuarial fairness' which involves the application of concepts of risk developed in the commercial world to health insurance. Clifford and Iulcano (1987) describe actuarial fairness as:

> policyholders with the same expected risk of loss should be treated equally . . . An insurance company has the responsibility to treat all its policyholders fairly by establishing premiums at a level consistent with the risk represented by each policyholder.

Actuarial fairness is often explained by reference to what Thomas Murray describes as the 'Lloyds of London Model':

> if two oil tanker companies ask to have their cargoes and vessels insured, one for a trip up the Atlantic to a US port, the other for a voyage through the Arabian Gulf during the height of the war in Kuwait and Iraq, the owner of the first ship would cry foul if she were charged the same extraordinarily high rate as the owner of the second (Murray, 1992).

One of the central issues of the whole debate is whether this mode of actuarial fairness should be applied to human beings seeking life or health insurance. Genetic testing skews this fairness principle, first because some will be aware of their risk status whereas others will not and secondly, because the risks associated with particular genotypes are not voluntarily assumed by individuals but are rather the result of the luck of the draw. Should these genetic differences be regarded in the same way as voluntarily assumed risks when the consequence of treating them differently is that those most in need of health care are most likely to be denied it? Miller makes a similar point:

> the use of genetic testing and test results by insurers raises important questions concerning the fairness of using an uncontrollable variable – genetic composition – to shift the economic burden of genetic disorders from the entire insured population to the unlucky person who has the defective genes (Miller, 1989).

6.6.1 The issue of fairness

The concept of actuarial fairness is subjected to close scrutiny by Daniels in an article examining the implications of insurance underwriting for HIV positive patients (Daniels, 1990). According to Daniels there is a confusion at the heart of the concept of actuarial fairness. He contends that difficulties arise when actuarial fairness comes to be considered as a normative rather than a descriptive construct. He states that the term actuarial fairness as used in the literature:

> expresses the moral judgment that fair underwriting practices must reflect the division of people according to the actuarially accurate determination of their risks (Daniels, 1990).

Daniels contends that underwriters are wrong to use the term 'fairness' in their description of their practices. The implication of using this phraseology is that there is something morally fair about stratification of risks among individuals. In fact, the interests of social justice may well require that such a practice be prohibited. Daniels' argument against risk segregation relates to the health insurance system in the United States. In essence he argues that access to health care is an essential means of ensuring equality of opportunity through the treatment and amelioration of injury and disease. Since equality of opportunity is regarded as a primary element of social justice, denial of health insurance consequently denies equality of opportunity and therefore frustrates social justice. This, of course, depends on the model of social justice which is adopted. For the sake of this discussion the models of social justice can be reduced to a bipolar discussion of what shall be styled libertarian Nozickian and liberal Rawlsian arguments.

6.6.2 The libertarian model

The libertarian Nozickian conception of social justice in the health care insurance context might be described as follows:

- individual differences between human beings can be regarded as an integral component of an individual's personal assets;
- individuals should have absolute liberty to profit or gain advantage from their personal assets;
- social arrangements will only be just in so far as they recognize individual differences as assets and allow individuals to profit from them;
- consequently, individuals are entitled to have markets structured for them in a manner that will allow them to maximize their personal advantages.

This strong libertarian argument supports the insurance company conception of moral fairness as actuarial fairness. Nozickian conceptions of social justice would regard community-rated insurance schemes as actuarially unfair as the extra premiums paid by those at a lower than average risk would in effect amount to the confiscation of property without consent (Nozick, 1974).

6.6.3 The liberal model

The liberal Rawlsian conception of social justice generates a somewhat different model. Under the 'veil of ignorance' individuals are prevented from having an awareness about their individual differences. A position which mirrors the state of knowledge about genetic health in the early days of genetic testing. Rawls theory attempts to define which individual differences should be considered relevant in the distribution of social goods such as health care and life insurance. Daniels points out that most Western democracies have, in fact, delineated certain areas of individual difference which are not to be used as determinants in the distribution of social goods. Race and sex are the classic examples. Legislation prohibiting discrimination based on sex, race and religion is now commonplace. Why are these particular features singled out as unacceptable bases for advantage and disadvantage? One feature which they all share is the fact that these characteristics are the result of a 'natural lottery' (Miller, 1989) in so far as they are predetermined and cannot be altered, except in some rare instances, by the autonomous action of the individual in question. The Rawlsian conception of social justice would rule that these characteristics should not be used in the classification of insurance risks because of the consequent denial of equal opportunity. Again Daniels observes that the reality of health-care systems throughout the world reflects the Rawlsian model rather than the Nozickian as they are based on a 'rejection of the view that individuals should have the opportunity to gain economic advantage from differences in their health risks' (Daniels, 1990).

From this, two central issues can be raised in an analysis of actuarial fairness. Firstly, the form of insurance under discussion must be scrutinized to determine what type of social good is being discussed. Is health insurance to be considered a primary social good? Is life insurance? These are crucial questions in determining the appropriate moral and legal responses in this area. A second issue which arises if it is determined that the insurance in question is to be considered a primary social good is whether or not it is acceptable to deny individuals access to that social good through the introduction of risk-rated practices where the features being identified in the risk segregation are themselves nonvoluntary such as race, sex or genetic characteristics.

6.6.4 Actuarial fairness and genetic testing

In order to determine the acceptability or otherwise of risk rating using genetic information the concept and practice of actuarial fairness can be explored further. Daniels argues that actuarial fairness as it is loosely described by the insurance industry can conceal one of three strategies. The first strategy would require underwriters to seek out all possible information about the risk in question. In the context of genetic information this would impose a positive duty on insurance companies to utilize all forms of available genetic testing, and on an extreme view, to require investment in research which would yield new forms of genetic test. A second strategy would require underwriters to use all relevant and available information about the risk in question. Thus the insurance company would seek out all existing genetic test information and utilize it where it was of value to do so. The third strategy of 'actuarial fairness' would be to allow underwriters to use information about a particular risk when it would be in their economic interests to do so. This would reflect a scenario where insurance companies considered an individual's genetic test results with a view to increasing the premium but would not consider the information as relevant to the reduction of the premium. Interestingly, some insurance products, such as preferred lives policies, reflect exactly this strategy where individuals are subjected to rigorous medical examinations in return for a reduction in premium. Andre Chuffart of Swiss Re Insurance has cautioned against these policies arguing that:

> The practical result of such an approach, however, is that for an increasing number of people i.e. those who do not qualify as preferred lives or those belonging to segments of the population which do not retain the interest of product development units, insurance may become more and more expensive, possibly unaffordable, or even unavailable (Chuffart, 1996).

One legislative strategy which has been established to frustrate this approach is the Belgian Law on Insurance Contracts which prohibits the use of genetic test information even where the results of the test are to the advantage of the proposer [4].

6.6.5 Industry strategies

Which of these three strategies is currently used by insurance companies in the context of genetic testing? The first is not currently employed. The relatively standard response of insurance companies throughout Europe is that they will not require genetic tests to be carried out in advance of a proposal. The ABI for example in their 1997 policy statement stated that: 'Applicants must not be asked to undergo a genetic test in order to obtain insurance.'

This is not the major concession it might at first appear. Genetic testing is expensive and since currently 95% of applicants can be risk rated from the information obtained from the proposal form, a requirement for genetic testing would not only be economically impractical but would be disproportionate. The degree to which the insurance industry is prepared to become actively involved either in the funding of research into genetic testing or into research into the quality and quantity of genetic testing available is surprisingly minimal. The United Kingdom Human Genetics Advisory Commission (HGAC) Subgroup on Insurance found that:

> the insurance industry generally does not have the information which would be needed to make actuarially sound use of genetic test results. Genetic test results become actuarially significant only if connected to medical and epidemiological research that establishes what health and life-span can be inferred from a given genetic test result and this generally requires substantial research.

The HGAC group found that the United Kingdom insurance industry had a relatively minimalist approach to this. There were very few companies which had access to either scientific research or to actuarial research based on scientific findings. Such an approach clearly raises the possibility that risk-rating decisions which are supposedly made on the basis of actuarial fairness will in fact be based on a limited knowledge of the scientific realities and consequently will not even be actuarially accurate (HGAC, 1997).

The second strategy of actuarial fairness, that of utilizing all relevant and material risk information, is the approach which the insurance industry would claim that it is currently using. Once again the ABI state in their recent Code of Practice that:

> Insurers may take account of existing genetic test results only when their reliability and relevance to the insurance product has been established (ABI, 1997b).

It is, however, the third strategy of actuarial fairness which most closely approximates to the reality of insurance practice emerging in the genetic age. This approach involves the utilization of risk information by insurance companies when it is in their economic interest so to do. Implicit in this strategy is the fact that risk information will not necessarily be utilized to the benefit of the insurance proposer. This would seem to undermine somewhat the claim that actuarial fairness is in fact morally fair because it simply seeks to accurately match risks to premiums.

6.7 THE CONCEPT OF ADVERSE SELECTION

Adverse selection is the converse side of the debate on actuarial fairness. Underwriters and the insurance industry are preoccupied with concerns about the possibility of adverse selection developing in the insurance market as a consequence of predictive genetic testing. Many of the strategies developed to ensure actuarial fairness are targeted at the danger of adverse or antiselection. The United States Actuarial Standards Board defines adverse selection as:

> The actions of individuals, acting for themselves or for others, who are motivated directly or indirectly, to take advantage of the risk classification system (Pokorski, 1996).

The United Kingdom HGAC Subgroup on Insurance described how:

> adverse selection can occur when the distribution of risk in a pool of insured people is skewed adversely, e.g. when more high risk people find it worthwhile to take out insurance. This drives up the price of premiums, so that low risk people may be deterred from taking out policies and may withdraw – this leads to a vicious circle of worsening of the risk pool and increasing costs (HGAC, 1997, p. 13).

The question of whether an increase in the use of genetic testing and the dissemination of genetic information to individuals will ultimately result in industry threatening adverse selection is a fiercely contested one. Insurance companies tend to argue that adverse selection in the context of genetic testing will severely threaten the viability of an open insurance market. Pokorski argues that:

> a staggering financial advantage can be attained when one party in a contractual agreement knows more than the other. Some people will attempt to use genetic test results to create an estate when none would have existed prior to testing . . . For many people the temptation to buy insurance in these circumstances will be irresistible. Simply stated, if life expectancy is much shorter than anticipated, purchasing life insurance at standard rates is the world's best financial investment (Pokorski, 1997).

The ABI relied on two precedents in their submission to the HGAC Subgroup on Insurance. They highlighted the adverse selection suffered in the 1980s when individuals who were aware that they were HIV positive took out insurance cover without disclosing their seropositivity. In addition, they raised the example of the 'mistake' made by some British insurance companies during the MIRAS crisis in 1983. These two examples are not particularly convincing evidence that the insurance industry can be destroyed by adverse selection. In both instances individuals did seek to play the insurance market using asymmetrical information for their own advantage but the market clearly had the capacity to absorb the economic impact of this activity.

MacDonald (1997) argues that three separate factors determine the nature and possibility of adverse selection in life insurance. The first factor is the rate at which insurance is purchased. If the rate of purchase is high then, according to MacDonald, the impact of a small number of adverse selectors will be minimal. The second factor is the rate at which people with a known risk factor, who therefore are potential adverse selectors, are likely to purchase insurance. The third factor is the extent to which these adverse selectors assure their lives for higher than normal amounts. MacDonald developed mathematical models in an attempt to predict the impact of genetic testing on the life insurance industry in terms of adverse selection. His conclusions are illuminating. If life insurance companies do not use the results of genetic tests in life insurance underwriting then additional costs will be incurred. However, MacDonald contends that these costs may be absorbable by the insurance industry if attention is paid to the third factor, namely limiting the possibility of adverse selectors purchasing unusually large policies. This can be done through the adoption of policy 'ceilings' which require more detailed information once the sum assured exceeds a predetermined level.

6.8 COMMUNITY-RATED UNDERWRITING

This is the method which originally underpinned the National Insurance system in the United Kingdom. Under such a system all policyholders' premiums are identical and the calculation of loss is based on what would be expected from a geographical area. Thus under the National Insurance system, all premiums were equal regardless of risk. The system of community rating reflects the concept of community responsibility for providing health care for its weaker members. Questions as to pre-existing conditions or the existence of certain risk factors such as smoking or alcohol consumption are considered irrelevant. In the United States some legislatures have begun enacting legislation to introduce a requirement that insurers set premiums on a community basis rather than assessing risk. There is more than a little irony in the fact that at the very time when the community-rated National Health Service (NHS) in the UK appears to be under threat from the increasing emphasis put on private provision, state legislatures in the private health economy of the US are enacting community rating schemes. In New York, a community-rating law was enacted in April 1993 which required that insurers establish community-rated premiums for health insurance sold directly to individuals and small groups [5]. Similarly in Maine an 'Act to Provide More Affordable Health Insurance for Small Businesses and Community Rating of Health Insurance Providers' was put into force in July 1993 [6]. One of the key questions to address in light of genetic diagnostic tests is which method of underwriting is most suited for both science and society.

NOTES

1. Great Republic Insurance Company memorandum excluding 'restaurant employees, antique dealers, interior decorators, fashion designers and florists'. See Schatz, B. (1987).
2. US PL 104-191 The Health Coverage Availability and Affordability Act 1996.
3. The American Council of Life Insurance gives a figure of 96% coverage in 1994.
4. Law of Non-Marine Insurance Contract 1992. Article 5. The Association of British Insurers have also stated that they will not allow the results of genetic tests to be used in the writing of 'preferred lives' insurance policies. 'Insurers must not offer individuals lower than standard premiums on the basis of their genetic test results, i.e. genetic test results will not be taken into account for preferred life underwriting.' (ABI, 1997b)
5. In Kass N. (1992) The rationale behind this legislation was outlined by the New York Assembly: 'The problems we are facing appear to be caused primarily by allowing the underwriting of health insurance risks and by the current statutory authority which allows community rating and experience rating to exist as competing rating methodologies . . . By permitting only community rating on an open enrolment basis . . . greater stability in premium rates should be achieved. By requiring open enrolment with only a pre-existing condition exclusion to protect insurers from adverse selection, more options for affordable coverage will be available.'
6. The Maine legislation phases in a requirement that insurers doing business in the state adopt community rating for small group health plans over four years.

REFERENCES

ABI (Association of British Insurers) (1997a) *Life Insurance and Genetics: A policy statement*. ABI, London.

ABI (Association of British Insurers) (1997b) *Code of Practice on Genetic Testing*. ABI, London.

Barr, N. (1993) *The Economics of the Welfare State,* 2nd Edn. Weidenfield & Nicholson, London.

Bartrum, T.E. (1993) Fear, discrimination and dying in the workplace: AIDS and the capping of employees health insurance benefits. *Kentucky Law J.* **82**: 249.

Bernstein, P.L. (1998) *Against the Gods: The Remarkable Story of Risk.* Wiley, New York, p.85.

Charatan, F.B. (1996) New Jersey passes genetic privacy bill. *BMJ* **71**: 313.

Chuffart, A. (1996) *Genetics and Life Insurance.* Swiss Re Publications,. Zurich.

Clifford, K.A. and Iulcano, R.P. (1987) AIDS and insurance: The rationale for AIDS-related testing. *Harvard Law Rev.* **100**: 1806.

Daniels, N. (1990) Insurability and the HIV epidemic: ethical issues in underwriting. *Milbank Q.* **68**: 497.

Doll, R. and Hill, A.B. (1950) Smoking and carcinoma of the lung: preliminary report. *BMJ.* **2**: 739–748.

Hennekens, C.H. (1998) Increasing burden of cardiovascular disease: current knowledge and future directions for research on relevant risk factors. *Circulation* **97**: 1095.

HGAC (Human Genetics Advisory Commission) (1997) *The Implications of Genetic Testing for Insurance*. HGAC, London.
Kass, N. (1992) Insurance for the insurers: the use of genetic tests. *Hastings Center Report* **22**: 6–10.
Leigh, S. (1990) Underwriting: a dying art? *J. Inst. Actuaries* **117**: 443.
Light, D.W. (1991) The ethics of corporate health insurance. *Business and Professional Ethics J.* **10**: 49.
Loue, S. (1993) An epidemiological framework for the formulation of health insurance policy. *J. Legal Med.* **14**: 523.
MacDonald, A.S. (1997) How will improved forecasts of individual lifetimes affect underwriting? *Br. Actuarial J.* **3**: 1009.
Miller, J.M. (1989) Genetic testing and insurance classification: National action can prevent discrimination based on the 'luck of the genetic draw'. *Dickinson Law Rev.* **93**: 729.
Mortenson, L.E. (1989) Starve them or shoot them. *Hastings Center Report* **19**: 3.
Murray, T.H. (1992) Genetics and the moral mission of health insurance. *Hastings Center Report* **22**: 15.
Nozick, R. (1974) *Anarchy, State & Utopia*. Basil Blackwell.
Ostrer, H., Allen, W., Crandell, L.A., Mosely, R., Dewar, M., Nye, D. and McCrary, S.V. (1993) Insurance and genetic testing: where are we now? *Am. J. Hum. Genet.* **52**: 565.
Padgug, R. (1991) Looking backward: Empire Blue Cross and Blue Shield as an object of historical analysis. *J. Health Politics, Policy and Law* **16**: 793.
Pokorski, R.J. (1996) Use of genetic tests to predict and diagnose cancer: An insurance perspective. *J. Tumor Marker Oncol.* **11**: 33.
Pokorski, R. (1997) Insurance underwriting in the genetic era. *Am. J. Hum. Genet.* **60**: 205–208.
Roscam-Abbing, H. (1991) Genetic predictive testing and private insurances. *Health Policy* **18**: 197.
Rothman, D.J. (1991) The public presentation of Blue Cross, 1935–1965. *J. Health Politics, Policy and Law* **16**: 671.
Schatz, B. (1987) The AIDS insurance crisis. Underwriting or overreaching? *Harvard Law Rev.* **100**: 1782.
US Office of Technology Assessment (1988) *AIDS and Health Insurance*. OTA, Washington DC.
Wilkie, A.D. (1997) Mutuality and solidarity: assessing risks and sharing losses. *Br. Actuarial J.* **3**: 986.

Chapter
7

INSURANCE, GENETICS AND THE LAW

Tony McGleenan

7.1 INTRODUCTION

The actuarial significance of genetic testing has led to various legislative initiatives which attempt to mitigate the potentially negative social consequences which could develop if predictive genetic tests become widely used in the formulation of insurance contracts. Genetic testing produces predictive information which is relevant from the perspective of risk rating. Accurate determination of risk is the central concern of mutuality-based insurance which charges premiums in proportion to risk or in some cases deems the risk too high for any form of coverage. The legal principles which regulate this business of risk classification have their roots in the beginnings of the modern insurance industry. This chapter examines the legal principles which surround the disclosure of information which is predictive of risk. It examines a number of models of disclosure which might promote fairness in the age of predictive genetic medicine. Having looked at the principles which have shaped the insurance industry the recent legislative initiatives which have been specifically directed at the problems of insurance and genetics are examined. Finally, the strategies which have been developed in the United States to address the dangers of genetic discrimination in a nation where primary social goods such as health care are funded through risk-rated mutual private insurance policies are considered.

7.2 DISCLOSURE

7.2.1 The principle of uberrimae fides

Insurance contracts are described in United Kingdom law as contracts *uberrimae fides* which means that these contracts must be made in the utmost good faith. In effect, this means that every material piece of information which is known to the proposer must be passed on to the insurer. Failure to pass on any such relevant information can result in the contract being declared void. This is more than a duty to answer questions truthfully. In effect it amounts to a positive duty of disclosure of all material facts (Hamilton, 1994). This duty is an ancient one which has underpinned insurance since its earliest days. It is well stated by Lord Mansfield in the eighteenth century case of *Carter* v. *Boehm:*

> 'Insurance is a contract upon speculation. The special facts upon which the contingent chance is to be computed, lie most commonly in the knowledge of the insured only: the underwriter trusts to his representation and proceeds upon the confidence that he does not keep back any circumstance in his knowledge, to mislead the underwriter into a belief that the circumstance does not exist, and to induce him to estimate the risque as if it did not exist (*Carter* v. *Boehm,* 1766).

A number of legal questions arise within this doctrine. The question of what constitutes materiality is one of them. This is resolved in United Kingdom Law by the provisions of the Marine Insurance Act which states in section 18(2) that:

> every circumstance is material which would influence the judgment of a prudent insurer in determining whether or not he will take the risk, and, if so, at what premium and on what conditions.

It has been argued by some, notably Murray (1992) and Daniels (1990), that principles of actuarial fairness developed to deal with the risks inherent in the world of maritime commerce are inappropriate for life and health insurance where something approximating more closely to moral fairness would be more appropriate. In United Kingdom law this line of reasoning has been authoritatively rejected by the Court of Appeal in *Lambert* v. *Co-operative Insurance Society* (1975). In that case the plaintiff signed a proposal form for an insurance policy to cover jewellery owned by herself and her husband. The plaintiff did not inform the insurance company that her husband had a previous conviction for receiving stolen goods. The contract stated that it would be declared void where there was an omission to state any fact material to estimating the risk. A claim was made following the theft of the jewellery and was rejected by the insurance company on the ground that the contract was void for nondisclosure. The Court of Appeal examined the law on disclosure and found that in theory there were four possible approaches to take to the issue of disclosure:

(i) to disclose only such facts as the insured believes to be material;
(ii) to disclose such facts as the reasonable man would believe to be material;
(iii) to disclose such facts as the particular insurer would regard as material;
(iv) to disclose such facts as a reasonable or prudent insurer would regard as material.

The Court found that the provisions of the Marine Insurance Act followed the fourth approach and rejected the argument that the rules of Marine

Insurance should not apply outside the context of shipping. Lord Justice Cairns held that 'there is no obvious reason why there should be a rule in marine insurance different from the rules in other forms of insurance and, in my opinion, there is no difference.' The matter was revisited in the 1984 case of *Container Transport International Inc* v. *Oceanus Mutual Underwriting Association* (1984) where the Court of Appeal ruled that it was not necessary to show that the failure to disclose the information would actually have affected the actuarial process either in the decision whether or not to underwrite or in the calculation of the relevant premium. This decision produced the somewhat bizarre result whereby a piece of information which an insurer will regard, in fact, as immaterial will be considered in law as material for the purposes of declaring the contract in question void. A system which is based around the duty of the proposer to disclose all materially relevant information to an insurer is not the only possible response. A number of different approaches have been adopted in other nations which may be more appropriate in the context of predictive genetic testing when individual proposers may not be in a position to determine the materiality of the information which their genetic test has revealed.

7.2.2 The reasonable insured model

The approach to disclosure which has been adopted in Australia, Belgium and Ireland (Greenford, 1994) is one where disclosure is required of all facts which appear material to the reasonable insured. This objective standard is arguably fairer to the insured party. This approach is contained in the Belgian Law on Insurance Contracts 1992 and also appears in the Australian Insurance Contracts Act. Section 21 of this legislation states that:

> (1) an insured has a duty to disclose to the insurer, before the relevant contract of insurance is entered into, every matter that is known to the insured being a matter that:
> (a) the insured knows to be a matter relevant to the decision of the insurer whether to accept the risk and, if so, on what terms; or
> (b) a reasonable person in the circumstances could be expected to know to be a matter so relevant.

This sets out in clear terms the duty of the proposer, but the Act also goes on to specify that which is not considered to be part of the duty of the proposer:

> (2) The duty of disclosure does not require the disclosure of a matter:
> (a) that diminishes the risk;
> (b) that is of common knowledge;
> (c) that the insurer knows or in the ordinary course of the insurer's business as an insurer ought to know.

It would seem that such a clear exposition of the rights and responsibilities of insurer and proposer would be particularly useful in cases where individual proposers may be in possession of genetic information. The problem of determining materiality is not simply related to the complexities of the technology nor to the opaque language used but to the basic conceptual confusions which exist as to what, in fact, can be considered genetic information and what, in fact, consitutes a genetic test. There is very little consensus on these issues despite the fact that a significant number of legislative provisions have attempted definitions of just these issues.

7.2.3 The reasonable response model

A slightly different but related approach to the issue of disclosure in insurance contracts is that which requires the proposer to volunteer a reasonable response to questions put by the insurer. This approach is followed in Finland, France and Switzerland. If the proposer fails to respond to a question then they can be considered to be in breach of the their duty to offer a reasonable response. Under the model the proposer must offer a reasonable and honest response to the questions which are put on the proposal form. The proposer is not entitled to conceal any information which a reasonable person would regard as relating to the assessment of risk. Obviously questions of extreme generality cannot be included in such a system. There are disadvantages with such an approach. Of necessity it involves the use of more complex and lengthy proposal forms which in turn will increase overheads and transaction costs.

7.2.4 The subjective proposer model

The English Law Commission considered a further model which might have application in the context of insurance and genetic technology. This model considers the disclosure which would be required of a reasonable man of the same educational and socioeconomic background as the proposer. It is not a pure subjective test but rather a qualified objective standard of what ought to be disclosed (Law Commission, 1979). This is an attempt to mitigate to some extent the unfairness which can result when policies are ruled to be void because of nondisclosure of facts which the individual in question could not conceivably have considered to be relevant. The obvious difficulty with this approach is that it can lead to uncertainty over the standards which will be applied in individual cases which is something that the insurance industry, in general terms, is wary of. However, such an approach promotes fairness towards the insured. In the context of genetic technology the questions which are asked in relation to the possession of genetic information must be carefully worded given the documented difficulties with public awareness of genetic concepts.

7.2.5 Proportionality

In France the Insurance Code introduces the element of proportionality into the determination of the appropriate degree of disclosure required in the formulation of insurance contracts and in the resolution of disputed insurance claims. The concept underpinning this approach is relatively straightforward. In instances where there is wilful misrepresentation of information which is actuarially important the insurance contract is held to be void. This approach ensures a degree of protection against the possibility of adverse selection. In circumstances where the nondisclosure is not wilful, where for example, a proposer failed to reveal the results of a prognostic test which they did not believe to be a genetic test as defined by the law, then in the event of a claim the insurer pays the proportion of the claim which the premium paid bears to the premium which would have been charged had full disclosure been made (Clarke, 1997). In other words if full disclosure of the information would have resulted in an actual premium which was 50% higher than the original premium then the policyholder should receive 50% of the payment when the claim is made. This pragmatic approach avoids the harshness of the rule which excludes any payment in circumstances where an honest mistake has been made. Given the definitional problems which arise in relation to terms such as 'genetic test' and 'genetic information' the possibility of such inadvertent nondisclosure cannot be discounted.

7.2.6 A duty to investigate

Some states manage to operate more or less in the absence of a specific obligation of disclosure in insurance contracts. Such a situation pertains in the United States where an insurer can avoid an insurance contract on the basis of nondisclosure where the information was not discovered by the insurers own investigation of the risk and where there has been wilful concealment on the part of the proposer. This approach puts the onus on the insurer to properly investigate the risks brought by a particular proposal but also protects the insurer from the dangers of fraud and adverse selection. Ultimately this approach moves the cost of acquiring risk information from the proposer to the insurer while shifting the ultimate cost of fraud onto the insurance pool as a whole. Arguably it is fairer to require risk assessment to be made by the expert in the insurance industry rather than to place that burden upon the proposer who will not have the same degree of expertise and who will ultimately bear the cost if an error is made.

7.3 LEGISLATIVE RESPONSES TO GENETICS AND INSURANCE

In recent years a significant number of states have enacted specific legislation or developed regulatory frameworks in an effort to prevent the acquisition of genetic information from impacting adversely on the insurance industry or on individual citizens who find that they are denied insurance coverage as a consequence of their genetic profile. There has been a remarkable divergence of approach among the various states who have sought to enact legally binding norms.

7.3.1 Norway

Norway passed legislation specifically addressing the issue of genetic testing and insurance contracts in the Act Relating to the Application of Biotechnology in Medicine in 1994. Section 6 of the Act states that genetic testing can only be performed for medical diagnostic or therapeutic purposes. The legislation expressly prohibits requesting, receiving, retaining or making use of genetic information relating to a third party if that information has been obtained as a result of a genetic test. This seems to leave open the possibility of the use of 'traditional' forms of genetic information, such as family pedigrees, while clearly prohibiting the use of genetic diagnostic tests.

7.3.2 The Netherlands

Current practice in the Netherlands is that Dutch insurance companies are prohibited by the terms of the Medical Examinations Act 1998 from seeking disclosure of the results of any genetic test where the amount being sought is less than NLG 300 000. The rationale behind the legislation is that individuals ought not to be denied access to basic social goods such as employment and basic insurance products. The legislative scheme therefore prohibits certain types of medical examination. An individual must not be asked whether he or she will suffer from any hereditary, untreatable or serious disease unless they are already expressing symptoms of the disease. In addition, the legislation attempts to prohibit the acquisition of genetic information through the results of relatives. Insurers are prohibited from asking whether any blood relative has any hereditary, serious, untreatable disease, even if the individual is exhibiting symptoms of that disease. For insurance policies with a value in excess of the threshold of NLG 300 000 for life insurance and NLG 60 000 for disability policies the insurance companies are at liberty to seek disclosure of existing genetic information, but not to require an individual to take a genetic test.

The approach adopted in the Netherlands is one which is in effect a relatively common practice in the insurance industry. A system which triggers requests for disclosure or examination is already well established for certain insurance products. *Table 1* (MacDonald, 1998) illustrates how policy ceilings are used in the United Kingdom to determine what level of underwriting investigation is required before a particular life is accepted.

Table 1. Typical underwriting policy ceilings

Age on next birthday	Medical report sum assured (£)	Medical examination sum assured (£)
0–40	120 000	300 000
41–50	100 000	200 000
51–55	75 000	125 000
56–60	40 000	75 000
61–65	15 000	25 000
66–75	All	All

Table 1 shows that individuals under the age of 40 can obtain life insurance up to a value of £120 000 without triggering a request for a medical report. A similar individual will be able to propose for life insurance up to a value of £300 000 without the need for a medical examination.

The use of this strategy for genetic conditions was formulated originally by the Dutch Health Council which is a scientific advisory board for the Dutch Government. The Council issued a report in 1989 which recommended that the requirement of genetic testing for insurance reasons should be prohibited. Where genetic information already existed then it should only be used when the coverage sought exceeded a certain amount. In adopting this strategy the Health Council was influenced by a number of factors. The Council felt that a compelled genetic test would constitute an excessive infringement of individual rights to self-determination, could violate the privacy of relatives and was unnecessary because the justification of the risk of adverse selection was absent (Roscam Abbing, 1991).

7.3.3 Belgium

Belgium was one of the first European states to enact legislation which specifically addresses the problem of genetic testing in insurance. The Belgian Law of Insurance Contracts was passed in 1992 and Article 5 states that:

> The policyholder is obliged to declare exactly, at the time of completing the contract, any particulars known to him or her which he or she could reasonably be expected to consider as constituting risk assessment elements for the insurer. However, he/she does not have to disclose details which are already known to the insurer or which the insurer should be reasonably expected to know. Genetic data cannot be transmitted.

This article prevents a proposer for life insurance from passing on details about their genotype. This includes situations where the proposer is seeking to pass on the information in order to secure a lower premium. Article 95 of the Law on Insurance Contracts is also relevant. It states that:

> The physicians nominated by the insured shall submit to the insured, at his or her request, the medical certificates necessary for the completion and execution

> of the contract. The medical examinations necessary for the completion and execution of the contract are only to be based on past medical history establishing the insurance applicant's present medical state and not on genetic analysis techniques capable of determining his or her future state of health.

An interesting question in relation to this point is whether it will impact on any predictive test which is indicative of an individual's 'future state of health'. If so then routine prognostic procedures such as cholesterol and hypertension readings cannot be used for insurance purposes even where the result of such information would be to the advantage of the proposer. The legislation does refer specifically to 'genetic analysis techniques' but as is frequently the case with such instruments there is no explicit definition of these techniques.

7.3.4 Austria

The Austrian *Genetechnik Law* was passed in 1994 and deals predominantly with the issues of gene therapy. The legislation imposes a number of conditions which require the strong informed consent of an individual in advance of a genetic test being carried out. Section 65 (2) states:

> genetic screening may only be carried out with the written consent of the patient who has been informed in advance of the type, extent and effectiveness of the genetic test.

This strict requirement for informed consent would seem to impose some limitations on the use by insurers of genetic testing. Even more significant from the perspective of genetics and insurance is section 67 which states that:

> it is forbidden for employers and insurers including their representatives and employees to obtain, request, accept or in any other way make use of the results of genetic analyses on their employees, candidates, policyholders or insurance applicants.

The actual impact of this legislation is examined at length in Chapter 8. It is apparent that there can be some degree of divergence between the stated law and actual practice in the case of such strong prohibitions.

7.3.5 Australia

As in the majority of European states it is the issue of life insurance which is of most significance to the Australian system, although as in states such as the United Kingdom the number of people taking out private health insurance is generally increasing with over 30% of the population having private health insurance in 1997. The underwriting practices in Australia closely reflect the patterns seen elsewhere in Europe (Otlowski, unpublished). According to the Life Investment and Superannuation Association of

Australia approximately 93% of life insurance applicants are insured at standard premiums, 5% of applicants are insured at higher premiums and 2% are excluded from insurance altogether. The legal position in Australia mimics that in the rest of the common law world where the principles of underwriting are underpinned by a reliance on the doctrines of *uberrimae fides*. These common law rules are restated in the provisions of s.13 of the Insurance Contracts Act 1984. Consequently there is a statutory duty upon the proposer to disclose all relevant information to the insurer.

One complicating factor which is emerging in Australia, as in a number of other states, is the introduction of disability discrimination legislation. The Disability and Discrimination Act 1992 contains a specific exemption for insurance in section 46 which states that it is not unlawful for a person to discriminate against another person on the ground of the other person's disability by refusing to offer, or altering the terms and conditions of a life insurance policy or any other policy. The caveat is that the decision which is *prima facie* discriminatory must be based on actuarial or statistical data on which it is reasonable for the insurer to rely, and that the discriminatory decision is itself reasonable having regard to the matter of the data and all of the other factors in the proposal. As in other states where disability discrimination law recognizes an exemption for insurance contracts, there is an implicit acceptance that although discrimination in a broad sense does occur in insurance contracts the law can only tolerate such practices where they are based on relevant data. In the context of genetic information this does not quite provide insurers with the freedom to act as they might wish. The information being used must be statistically and actuarially relevant to the proposal in question. The difficulty which flows from this is in determining when genetic test results can be considered to be reliable enough in order to satisfy this test. The same questions arise in this context as have arisen in other jurisdictions. How is the standard of proof to be set in these cases? Who is to determine the reliability of the genetics tests? Will it be insurance companies, independent scientists, the pharmaceutical companies who develop and market the test (who are unlikely to be prepared to testify as to the unreliability of their product)? These matters are not addressed in the Australian legislation as they are similarly not addressed in many of the other states which seek to provide exemptions from discrimination laws for insurance companies. It is not simply the case that the reliability of genetic tests is in many cases questionable. There is the added issue that many of the tests are actually for multifactorial disorders where the test can do little more than indicate the probability that an individual has a predisposition to a particular disorder. The tested individual may modify their lifestyle in such a way as to avoid the disorder altogether or alternatively they may develop the disorder but at a level of severity which does not impinge in any relevant way on their actual lifestyle. Real risks of discrimination and injustice lie within these facts. Genetic information is complex and difficult even for experienced practitioners to deal with, where this information is being utilized in life insurance contracts simply by the administrative processing of the individual proposer's form then concerns about misinterpretation of genetic information clearly have real validity.

7.3.6 United Kingdom

The response of the United Kingdom government to issues such as genetic technology in recent years has been to adopt a strategy of procedural regulation. This trend can be seen in a number of areas from embryo experimentation to human gene therapy where reflexive regulatory structures have been put in place in order to address the challenges posed by fast-moving technological developments which have significant social ramifications (McGleenan, 1997). This has been equally true of the area of genetic and insurance. Following the recommendations of the House of Commons Select Committee on Science and Technology the government acted to establish a HGAC in 1997. This body immediately placed genetic testing and life insurance at the top of their agenda. Subsequently a framework of procedural regulation of genetics and insurance has been developed. Since this approach is one which has attracted a significant degree of interest it repays examination in some detail.

The Human Genetics Advisory Commission Report. One of the first acts of the Human Genetic Advisory Commission was the establishment of a subgroup to investigate the issues surrounding genetic testing and life insurance in the United Kingdom. This body published a report entitled *The Implications of Genetic Testing for Insurance* which found, *inter alia*, that a permanent ban on the use of genetic tests in insurance would be inappropriate. One reason advanced for this conclusion was that genetic testing technology is at such an early stage that it is unlikely that any actuarially important information will currently be generated by tests for multifactorial diseases. The report considered the question of adverse selection based on genetic test results and acknowledged that the empirical realities of adverse selection are strongly disputed. It also states that the life insurance industry could currently withstand the limited amount of adverse selection which would result as a consequence of nondisclosure of genetic test results. The report found that there are strong public concerns about the possibility of genetic discrimination but made no particularly firm recommendations on discrimination other than that the matter should be kept under review by the HGAC. The issue of disclosure of genetic test results was also addressed. The Commission recommends that 'for the time being the insurance industry should respect a moratorium on requiring the disclosure of results of genetic tests'. However, in a preceding paragraph it states that

> a requirement to disclose results of specific genetic tests as a condition of purchasing a specific type of insurance product would only be acceptable when a quantifiable association between a given pattern of test results and events actuarially relevant for a specific insurance product has been established.

This is effectively a restatement of conventional insurance principles. The insurance industry operates on the contractual basis that all materially relevant information must be disclosed. If such information is not disclosed then the contract in question is voidable. To say that the insurance industry should only be permitted to disclose information where there is a 'quantifiable association' between the test result and the actuarial utility of the information simply affirms the practice of the insurance industry. A more novel recommendation is that the government should establish a mechanism whereby the insurance industry would first have to prove that a lifting of the moratorium on requiring genetic test disclosure was justified. According to the report the burden of proof would only be discharged in such an instance where the connection between specific genetic test results and 'actuarially relevant events' was established by research published in peer-reviewed journals.

Association of British Insurers' Report. The Association of British Insurers (ABI) is the body which represents over 440 insurance companies in the United Kingdom. Between them these companies can account for over 95% of the insurance business transacted within the United Kingdom. The ABI also published a Genetic Testing Code of Practice in December 1997 which is to be fully reviewed at least once per year. The Code establishes a number of key principles for insurers. Paragraph 2 of the Code states that:

> applicants must not be asked to undergo a Genetic Test in order to obtain insurance.

Some of the clauses of the Report would seem to have benefited from crossfertilization of ideas contained within the HGAC document. For example, in a clause which seems to closely reflect some of the thinking outlined by the HGAC report the Code of Practice states at paragraph 4 that:

> Insurers may take account of existing Genetic Test results only when their reliability and relevance to the insurance product has been established.

The ABI Code states that genetic information may be used to increase insurance premiums although the Code points out that this will not necessarily be done in practice. The document clearly prohibits the use of genetic information for preferred life underwriting. Thus, although genetic testing information may, in restricted circumstances, be used to charge an increased premium, it will definitely not be used to set a lower premium where evidence of a decreased risk has been obtained through genetic testing. This marks a clear departure from general underwriting practice which attempts to precisely correlate the premium with the risk posed. In this instance the ABI considered that a break with traditional underwriting practice was justified because:

> insurers consider it necessary to allay public concern that an uninsurable genetic underclass may develop if the insurance industry were to seek out the 'good' genetic risks by offering them cheaper insurance.

Paragraph 11 of the Code of Practice anticipates the provisions of the new Data Protection Act 1998 (itself based on the European Privacy Directive) by requiring that the insurer must obtain the applicant's informed consent before processing any information obtained as a consequence of a genetic test result. The insurance company must explicitly state the purpose for which disclosure of the genetic test result is sought (presumably for underwriting purposes) and the information must not be used for anything other than these purposes. The Code goes on to attempt to allay one of the major concerns in relation to insurance and genetics, namely, the fear that information obtained as a consequence of one person's genetic test disclosure will be used in the computation of a related family member's premium. The Code explicity prohibits such a practice. Paragraphs 18–20 of the document establish a novel appeals process which can be utilized by dissatisfied insurance applicants. The recommendations of the HGAC report are reflected in the section of the ABI Code of Practice which deals with underwriting. The ABI states that a genetic test result may only affect the underwriting decision if it is reliable. The standard of reliability indicated is that the test must be either in use by the NHS or be validated by an expert body. In addition, the test in question must be deemed to be relevant to the insurance product. The implication seems to be that the question of relevance is to be determined by the ABI Genetics Adviser. The Code states that the only tests which are to be deemed reliable are single gene tests validated for service use in the NHS.

Part 4 of the Code contains a comprehensive description of the legal practice and procedure to be adopted by the three-person adjudication tribunal which will hear complaints from dissatisfied insurance applicants. The tribunal members are to be drawn from three separate registers of legally qualified professionals, insurance industry professionals and genetic science professionals. The adjudication process will be triggered when a complainant issues a formal Notice of Complaint having first exhausted the internal complaints procedure of the company in question. The insurance company is then required to make a formal Response to the Notice. When the issues between the parties have crystallized, an informal hearing will take place. As is the case with most tribunals legal representation is optional. The document states that the tribunal should be conducted in such a way as to make it possible to conduct cases without legal representation. Experience in other spheres where a tribunal system operates tends to indicate that the need for legal representation is dictated by the strategy adopted by 'repeat players': in this case the insurance company concerned. The fact that the tribunal will not be bound by its previous decisions may lessen the pressure on the insurance companies to use all available means to ensure that a binding decision does not go against them and consequently may reduce the need for costly legal representation. The possibility of an appeal from the decision of a tribunal is not explicitly addressed in the Code and it is generally unclear how this system is to fit with the civil legal system.

The United Kingdom Government Response: GAIC. The United Kingdom government considered the recommendations made by the Human Genetics Advisory Committee and the Code of Practice of the Association of British Insurers and issued a formal response in October 1998 (DTIOST, 1998). The response contains some important points although it falls short of introducing any form of prescriptive legislation. Firstly, it states that the government does not favor the continuance of a moratorium on the use of genetic information in insurance. The response states that:

> The Government concurs with the HGAC that a permanent ban on the use of genetic test results would not be appropriate.

The reasoning used to justify this rejection of the moratoria solution is that there will be circumstances where the results of genetic tests can in fact be used to the advantage of the applicant, presumably to secure a lower premium or to obtain insurance in circumstances where it would have otherwise been refused. It is notable that this argument has been rejected in a number of other jurisdictions. In Belgium and Norway for example, the use of genetic test results is forbidden even in circumstances where it will be to the advantage of the applicant.

However, the United Kingdom government did feel that some form of control should be exercised over the use of genetic information by the insurance industry. The ABI in their Code of Practice had suggested that the use of genetic tests should be limited by their reliability. The question of the validity and reliability of the tests to be used was to be determined according to either peer review in the science community or to the opinion of the genetics adviser. This suggestion raised obvious concerns about conflicts of interest and impartiality. The United Kingdom government responds to these concerns by calling for the establishment of a permanent independent evaluation mechanism to:

> evaluate the reliability and actuarial evidence relating to the use of specific genetic tests by insurers.

It is envisaged that approval by this body will be a prerequisite for the use of test results by the insurance industry. An exception to this prerequisite is the situation where a negative test result would operate in favor of the applicant.

In addition to this mechanism the government also believes that it is essential that a robust independent appeals mechanism should be established to facilitate aggrieved proposers who feel that genetic information has been inappropriately used in relation to their application. Once again this has clearly been influenced by the ABI Code of Practice which envisaged the setting up of a Tribunal system. The criticism leveled at that proposal was that it was not an independent mechanism (McGleenan, 1998). Aside from these concrete proposals there are a number of other interesting features of the United Kingdom government response. There is some hint of the philosophical approach to the concept of insurance where it is stated that:

> It is a matter of *public interest* that insurers continue an inclusive approach to insurance cover, where no individuals are excluded without good reason.

One interpretation of this comment might be that it could therefore be concluded that the government considers it to be in the public interest that people should be excluded from insurance where there is a good reason for so doing. This seems a rather unusual approach. Although it is undoubtedly in the interests of the insurance companies that bad risks are excluded, to conflate the industry interests with the public interest is a contentious argument particularly when the excluded risks may well call on the public purse to finance the social goods denied them as a result of their rejection. This rejection of an approach to insurance and genetic testing grounded on a theory and commitment to concepts of social solidarity is underlined in the government discussion of the concept of 'unfair discrimination' in paragraph 10 of the report where it is stated that:

> The Government is committed to ensuring that unfair discrimination by insurers does not occur. It notes that the HGAC were unable to find any definite evidence of unfair discrimination at present.

Once again an inference which might legitimately be drawn here is that the government view is that there are certain instances where discrimination against individuals based on the results of a genetic test can be considered fair.

The final stage of this procedural system of regulation of genetic technology and insurance was set in place in April 1999 with the establishment of the Genetics and Insurance Committee (GAIC). This is a nonstatutory advisory body which informs policy at the Department of Health (DoH, 1999). This committee has a primary function of developing mechanisms for assessing genetic tests and the use of their results by the insurance industry. Specifically the terms of reference of the committee state that it is to:

> develop and publish criteria for the evaluation of specific genetic tests, their application to particular conditions and their relevance and reliability to particular types of insurance; to report to Health, Treasury and Trade and Industry Ministers on proposals received by GAIC from insurance providers and the subsequent level of compliance by the industry with the recommendations of GAIC.

The United Kingdom response to the challenges of genetics and insurance represents the paradigm example of a soft or procedural regulatory framework. The responsivity of such an approach can be attractive in a dynamic area such as genetic technology but the countervailing uncertainty can pose problems particularly in an area such as insurance which trades on minimizing risk.

7.4 REGULATION OF INSURANCE LAW AND GENETICS IN THE UNITED STATES

There are a number of significant differences between the situation in the United States and that which pertains in Europe as recently argued by Wilkie (1998). He points out that:

> Genetic testing is a serious issue of public policy in the USA because so many of the population depend on private insurance contracts for their healthcare provision. In Britain, on the other hand, the entire populace can obtain medical care free at the point of delivery through the National Health Service.

What is true of the United Kingdom is true of most European states which have a socialized system of health care provision. As described by Husted in Chapter 1 the provision of health care in Europe is founded on the principle of social solidarity. In the United States health-care insurance is based on the entirely different concept of mutuality. The ramifications of this difference are quite simply that an insurance system based on mutuality must accurately classify the risks which individual proposers bring to the fund. In an era of predictive medicine this means that private insurance companies will seek to know the results of genetic tests, and may indeed, in some instances seek to encourage applicants to take such tests. These differences are also important from the perspective of policy. A series of federal and state bills have been brought forward in an effort to mitigate the harsh social consequences that may result from the widespread collection of genetic information. These laws do not necessarily serve as practical models for legislation in Europe because of the differing pattern of social and private insurance. They do, however, provide a valuable insight into the different approaches that can be taken to regulating genetics and insurance and also illustrate the potential difficulties which arise from such a course.

7.4.1 The problem of definition

One of the problems facing those who seek to restrict the use of genetic information or the use of genetic test results is the difficulty of defining what, in fact, amounts to genetic information and what amounts to a genetic test. The difficulties arise because the distinction as it is currently understood is based on questions of scientific methodology rather than on the inherent nature of the information itself. It would seem, however, that searching for a distinction between genetic and nongenetic may ultimately prove to be a futile exercise. There may come a point when all medically related information will be considered genetic. The important issue is not the classification of the information but rather whether or not it is reliably predictive of risk. In terms of the interaction between genetic information and the insurance industry, which has been the source of much concern, the origin of the information matters much less than whether it is prognostically reliable to a standard considered to be actuarially relevant. The actual scientific techniques used to obtain health-care information vary widely and there are clearly technical distinctions between taking a family history and taking samples of deoxyribonucleic acid (DNA). Yet, aside from the technological differences the consequences of both interventions is potentially identical. It does not necessarily matter whether the information is obtained by DNA analysis or by a lifestyle questionnaire because the significance of the information will be determined by its accuracy and predictive power. Attempts to protect individuals by restricting the use that can be made of genetic information are likely to be very limited in their utility because of the imprecision of language and the ever-changing nature of the technology. A more viable strategy may be to attempt to mitigate the negative effects of widely available accurate predictive medical information. Currently the responses adopted by many legislatures to the perceived dangers of widespread genetic testing are focused on the genetic dimension of the information. There is a perception that restricting the use of certain types of information obtained 'genetically' will keep the dangers of genetic discrimination at bay. Yet this approach misses the point that the scientific methodology used to obtain the information is not the cause of the problem, rather it is the negative social consequences which are likely to flow from the application of the existing systems of insurance and insurance law to powerfully predictive information.

7.4.2 State legislation

The United States experience is particularly instructive in this regard. A large number of states have sought to introduce legislation which prohibits insurers from seeking the results of genetic tests or from compelling individuals to take genetic tests. In January 1999 a bill was introduced into the Rhode Island assembly which sought to prevent health insurers from seeking a genetic test or the results of such a test. The definition of the genetic test was:

> a test of a person's genes, gene products, or chromosomes for abnormalities or deficiencies, including carrier status, that are linked to physical or mental disorders or impairments, or that indicate the presence of, or a susceptibility to, illness, disease, impairment or other disorders, whether physical or mental, or that demonstrate genetic or chromosomal damage due to environmental factors.

This definition would seem to be broad enough to include many routine diagnostic procedures since most will demonstrate in one form or another anomalous indicators based on genetic, chromosomal or environmental factors. A similar bill was introduced in the Florida House of Representatives in 1997. It defines a genetic test as:

> a test to determine the presence of mutations or variations in an individual's DNA. Genetic testing does not include routine physical examinations; chemical, blood and urine analysis; tests for abuse of drugs; and tests for the presence of the human immunodeficiency virus.

The inherent contradictions in this definition serve to underline the recurrent problem of defining the notion of a genetic test narrowly enough. It is difficult to form a conceptual argument which illustrates how a test for HIV is not an investigation into 'the presence of mutations or variation in an individual's DNA'. In Arizona, state law has been amended to prevent unfair discrimination by health insurers. Insurance companies are prohibited from refusing to consider an application for life or disability insurance on the basis of a genetic condition, developmental delay or developmental disability. A genetic test in that Code is defined as:

> an analysis of an individual's DNA, gene products or chromosomes that indicates a propensity for or susceptibility to illness, disease, impairment or other disorders, whether physical or mental, or that demonstrates genetic or chromosomal damage due to environmental factors, or carrier status for disease or disorder.

In Georgia, Senate Bill 233 amends Title 31 of the Code to prohibit accident and sickness insurers from using information derived from genetic testing to deny access to coverage. The Bill defines genetic tests as:

> laboratory tests of human DNA chromosomes for the purpose of identifying the presence or absence of inherited alterations in genetic material or genes which are associated with a disease or illness that is asymptomatic at the time of testing and that arises solely as a result of such abnormality in genes or genetic material.

As in other jurisdictions an attempt is here made to distinguish genetic tests from 'traditional' forms of predictive diagnostic medicine. The Georgia law states that the provisions are not intended to include routine physical measurements, chemical, blood or urine analysis, drug abuse tests and HIV tests. In Kentucky legislation was introduced by House Bill 315 in 1998 to prevent health insurers from excluding individuals or fixing premium rates on the basis of any genetic characteristic. The term genetic characteristic is defined as:

> any inherited gene or chromosome, or alteration that is scientifically or medically believed to predispose an individual to a disease, disorder or syndrome, or to be associated with a statistically significant increased risk of development of a disease, disorder or syndrome.

It is difficult to see what illnesses or disease such a definition would actually exclude. There is an obvious danger that once litigation on these issues begins to occur, as it inevitably must, the problems of interpretation will render the protections afforded by a prohibition on information generated by genetic tests almost completely meaningless. The Kentucky bill also extends to life insurance and makes it unlawful to discriminate against individuals on the basis of a genetic test or genetic information in the 'issuance, witholding, extension, renewal, underwriting of, or determining insurability for' life insurance. In Maine s.2159 of the Insurance Code expressly prohibits discrimination on the basis of genetic testing. The prohibition is confined to 'unfair discrimination' which is characterized as the application of genetic test results in a manner 'not reasonably related to anticipated claims experience'. This is an effort to introduce the concept of actuarial relevance into the regulation of genetics and insurance.

The issue of genetic discrimination has been examined in detail by Launis in Chapter 3 but the notion of 'unfair discrimination' is one which recurs frequently in discussions of genetics and insurance. The United Kingdom government has described the concept of 'unfair discrimination' (DTIOST, 1998) in a recent response to the Human Genetics Advisory Committee. The implication is that there is a category of fair discrimination. A recent editorial in the journal *Nature* argues that:

> in the end, both insurer and policyholder will have to share information equitably – there is no long-term alternative to consensual discrimination (Editorial, 1996).

This is a further example of a benign qualification being placed on the concept of discrimination which has until recently at least been, as Pokorski (1997) points out: 'the most feared epithet of an egalitarian society'. There is clearly a sense in which those who strongly support the maintenance of a risk-rated insurance system wish to distance themselves as far as possible from the concept of discrimination. There are obvious public relations reasons for so doing. But a central issue remains. Does treating someone less favorably in terms of insurance cover as a consequence of genetic information amount to discrimination?

A Bill entitled the Genetic Information Nondiscrimination in Health Insurance Act was introduced in the General Assembly of Maryland in

1998. It attempts to prevent insurance companies, nonprofit health care plans or health maintenance organizations from using 'a genetic test or the results of a genetic test, genetic information or a request for genetic services, to reject, deny, limit, cancel, refuse to renew, increase the rates of, affect the terms or conditions of, or otherwise affect a health insurance policy.' Once again the definition of genetic test is different from those which have been developed elsewhere and is rather broad in scope:

> a laboratory test of human chromosomes, genes or gene products that is used to identify the presence or absence of inherited or congenital alterations in genetic material that are associated with disease or illness.

Alongside the antidiscrimination strategy another method of offering protection against the social consequences of insurance is to prohibit the use of genetic information without the consent of the individual. This is the approach which is used in the Genetic Information Nondiscrimination in Health Insurance Act which is one of a number of federal bills introduced to address this issue. This particular measure was introduced in the United States Congress by Representative Slaughter in 1997. The proposal prohibits insurance providers from denying or cancelling health insurance coverage, or varying the terms and conditions of health insurance coverage, on the basis of genetic information, from requesting or requiring an individual to disclose genetic information without written prior consent. The Florida legislation adopts a similar approach and explicitly spells out the nature of the information which must be provided before the consent will be considered to be informed. The person taking a genetic test must be told that the test results could be inconclusive, that they could preclude the person from obtaining life or disability insurance and could restrict them from certain areas of employment. This form of legislation uses the autonomy of the individual as the regulatory lever, if an autonomous individual is fully appraised of the risks and benefits when they freely exercise their choice to accept or refuse a genetic test. The difficulty is that the freedom of choice in this context may be constrained by numerous factors. Reliance on individual autonomy in such circumstances may not prevent unwanted social consequences.

To date well over thirty American states have enacted or pending legislation relating in one way or another to genetics and insurance (Davis and Mitrius, 1996). The examples examined here are not an exhaustive list but have been selected to illustrate the different approaches that can be taken and the fundamental problems of definition which repeatedly occur. A further notable feature of much of the legislation passed or pending in the United States is the variability, or in many cases, absence of sanctions. Without strong civil sanctions wealthy corporations such as insurance companies may not be unduly troubled by state legislative provisions.

7.5 CONCLUSION

One obvious question which must arise at this point is whether the law can provide a solution to the problems of insurance and genetics. It can be said with some certainty that legislation cannot resolve or prevent the physiological suffering of those who have a genetic profile which predisposes them to genetic disease. However, such individuals may also suffer in an extra corporeal sense through the denial of primary social goods which are predicated upon an externalization of risks to insurance companies. It is within this narrow frame that law may be able to offer some palliation. The negative social consequences which may flow from genetic information are the result of legal and legislative constructs such as the duty of disclosure and doctrine of *uberrimae fides*. These legal principles were developed in order to secure mutual benefit by accurately classifying risk and preventing fraud and adverse selection. It is apparent that if it is agreed that these principles are producing unfair and adverse social consequences when operated in an environment rich in predictive medical information then they can be altered.

REFERENCES

Carter* v. *Boehm (1766) 3 Burr 1905.

Clarke, M. (1997) *Policies and Perceptions of Insurance.* Oxford University Press, Oxford.

Container Transport International* v. *Oceanus Mutual Underwriting Association (1984) 1 Lloyd's Report 476.

Daniels, N. (1990) Insurability and the HIV epidemic: ethical issues in underwriting. *The Milbank Quarterly* **68**: 497.

Davis, H.R. and Mitrius, J.V. (1996) Recent legislation on genetics and insurance. *Jurimetrics* **37**: 69.

DOH (Department of Health) (1999) Press release 1999/0235, 15 April 1999.

DTIOST (Department of Trade and Industry Office of Science and Technology) (1998) *Government Response to the Human Genetics Advisory Commission's Report on The Implications of Genetic Testing for Insurance*. DTI/Pub 3744/0.5k/10/98/NP.

Dutch Health Council (1989) *Genetics, Science & Society*. Dutch Health Council, The Hague.

Editorial (1996) *Nature* **379**: 379.

Greenford, B.C. (1994) Non-disclosure in Ireland. *Insurance Law and Property* **4**: 39

Hamilton, J. (1994) The duty of disclosure in the law of insurance *Juridical Rev*. 97.

Lambert* v. *Co-operative Insurance Society (1975) 2 Lloyd's Reports 485.

Law Commission (1979) *Working Paper No. 73.*

MacDonald, A. (1998) How will improved forecasts of individual lifetimes affect underwriting. *Philos. Trans.* **352**: 1067.

McGleenan, T. (1997) Legal regulation of genetic technology in the United Kingdom: hard or soft options. In: *Interdisciplinary Approaches to Gene Therapy: Legal,*

Ethical and Scientific Aspects (eds S. Muller, J. Simon and J.W. Westing) Springer Verlag, Heidelburg, pp. 1–18.

McGleenan, T. (1998) Insurance and genetics: recent developments in the United Kingdom. *Euroscreen Newsletter* **7**: 1.

Murray, T.H. (1992) Genetics and the moral mission of health insurance. *Hastings Center Report* **22**: 15.

Otlowski, M. *Implications of the Human Genome Project for Australian Law & Practice*. Discussion paper (unpublished).

Pokorski, R. (1997) Insurance underwriting in the genetic era. *Am. J. Hum. Genet.* **60**: 205.

Roscam Abbing, H. (1991) Genetic predictive testing and private insurances. *Health Policy* **18**: 197.

Wilkie, T. (1998) Genetics and insurance in Britain: why more than just the Atlantic divides the English-speaking nations. *Nature Genet.* **20**: 119.

Chapter
8

THE IMPLICATIONS OF GENETIC REGULATION FOR INSURANCE: THE AUSTRIAN EXPERIENCE

Gertrud Hauser and Astrid Jenisch

8.1 INTRODUCTION

Concern about the use and potential abuse of genetic information by insurers and employers has led to the drafting of a number of transnational and national legal instruments which seek to regulate the use of genetic information. At the transnational level measures such as that of the Council of Europe Convention on Biomedicine have appeared. This states *inter alia* that:

> Tests which are predictive of genetic diseases or which serve either to identify the subject as a carrier of a gene responsible for a disease or to detect a genetic predisposition or susceptibility to a disease may be performed only for health purposes or for scientific research linked to health purposes, and subject to appropriate genetic counselling. (Council of Europe, 1997)

At a national level Austria was one of the first European states to introduce legislation specifically aimed at addressing concerns relating to genetic technology. The Gene Technique Law was passed in 1994 and addresses a broad spectrum of interventions which incorporate recombinant DNA technology. In particular the legislation addresses the use of genetic information stating that it is prohibited to 'obtain, request, take or otherwise use results of gene analyses'. Consequently, developments in Austria since the passing of this law provide us with a unique insight into how a relatively strict regulatory regime will affect the insurance industry.

8.2 THE AUSTRIAN INSURANCE SYSTEM

In Austria there is a dual system of insurance. First, there is the social security state system which operates according to public law but is administered independently of the state, and so is in an intermediate position between private and direct state insurance. Secondly, there are private insurance companies. Both of these systems deal with retirement pension, health insurance and accident insurance. Life insurance (Erleben and Ableben), and dread disease (stroke, heart attack, multiple sclerosis etc.) insurance are only covered by private insurance companies.

8.2.1 The public insurance system

The public system of health insurance lays great importance on prevention, and covers antenatal care, neonatal care and medical examinations of young people and adults. Prevention also includes the possibility of genetic examination which covers genetic counseling, prenatal diagnosis, and cytogenetic investigation. In some cases these are automatic, after a doctor's recommendation for prenatal cytogenetic investigation in women over 36 years old. In others they are only available subject to approval of the doctor's recommendation by the chief social security medical officer. This category covers genetic testing by molecular methods. Just as the results of clinical examination of an employee are confidential and are not passed on to the employer, so too the results of these genetic investigations are also confidential (see Austrian Federal Law 510, 1994).

8.2.2 The private insurance system

There are several differences between the state and the private sector. From the point of view of the insured the principal difference is that whereas in the social security system contributions are fixed according to earnings (but may be voluntarily increased) and are compulsory, in the private system participation is entirely voluntary and the applicant chooses the amount that she/he wishes and is able to pay.

From the point of view of the insurer the key difference is that the state system does not refuse cover to any applicant, whereas the private companies are able to refuse to grant cover or only grant it at the cost of an increased premium. For the majority of insurance types information on the health status of the applicant is requested by the private insurer. Standard insurance proposal forms have for many years asked about recent medical treatment as well as relevant elements of family history (Harper, 1993). On the basis of the answers to standard questions the risk is categorized. Mortality statistics for different age groups in the population as a whole provide the basis for the actuarial calculation for life insurance premiums but these differ with sex, smoking and other relevant variables. Deaths from genetic disease as a whole are already included in the general mortality risk. From the point of view of the insurance company the genetic status of an applicant can be seen as a relevant variable if the presence of a gene for a particular disease denotes that the individual will die from or develop a disease by a specified age. There thus appears to be a conflict here between the interests of the insurer and the Gene Technique Law. So to what extent do the insurance companies comply? Enquiries have been made in Austria as to whether or not applicants in whom there may be a genetic problem would be accepted by an insurance company and on what terms. Some examples are set out in *Tables 1* and *2*.

8.3 INSURING GENETIC RISKS

Let us explain the results shown in the tables. Just as there is great variety in genetic diseases and their manifestations there is variety in the ways in which they are dealt with by the private insurance companies according to whether the applicant requires life, health or accident insurance. However, a characteristic feature of all such health policies is that they exclude any pathological manifestation connected with the primary condition in the applicant, referred to below as 'with exclusion'.

The premium to be paid consists of two parts: a general part taking into account risks from all other sources, and a part relating to the additional risk specific to the condition. The latter part may be weighted by a risk factor, the approximate upper limits for which are shown in *Tables 1* and *2* for different conditions. This may vary slightly from one company to another. In difficult cases with a high sum insured the insurance company may refer the question to their reinsurance company.

Among the chromosomal disorders patients with Down syndrome are the most common; they would be considered for life insurance as children but not before they are one year old, and cover would not extend beyond the age of 40–50 years. They would be considered for health insurance without any increased premium for covering pathological conditions excluding those connected with this syndrome, e.g. heart disease. They would not be considered for accident insurance. Applicants with Kleinfelter's disease with its variability of expression would be considered for life cover but there would be an increased premium payable. The excess would be based on an additional risk factor of up to 60%, depending on the severity of the condition in the patient. They would be considered for health insurance except for associated conditions, and would be eligible for accident cover except for those patients with mental handicap. Applicants with Turner syndrome would be considered for life and accident insurance without any restrictions and for health insurance 'with exclusion'. For these chromosome conditions the diagnosis is usually available at the time of application for insurance; if it is not then they would be treated as normal applicants who, especially if the sum insured is high, are referred for medical examination.

Table 1. Insurance policies for applicants with manifest genetic disorders (health policies exclude any pathological manifestation connected with the primary condition in the applicant, referred to below as 'with exclusion')

Syndrome	Life insurance	Health insurance	Accident insurance
Huntington's chorea	Not available	Available 'with exclusion'	Not available
Friedreich's ataxia	Available from 25 years onwards in light cases with risk 200–300%; not available if severe	Available 'with exclusion' Available 'with exclusion' Available 'with exclusion' or with high risk	Not available Not available Not available
Mucoviscidosis	Available only after 21 years; with 500–700% risk between age 21 and 35; after 35 years, 300–400% risk	Not available Not available Not available	Available Available Available
Down syndrome	Available but excludes infants and older adults (>40–50 years); risk depends on additional pathologies	Not available or available with high risk	Not available
Klinefelter	Available in light cases with moderate risk	Available 'with exclusion'	Available
Turner	Available if no pathologies; with pathologies, moderate risk	Available 'with exclusion' Available 'with exclusion'	Available Available
Hereditary hemosiderosis	Not available if severe; if light, available with 75–150% risk	Not available Available 'with exclusion'	Available Available
Muscular dystrophies:			
Duchenne	Not available	Not available	Not available
Facioscapulohumeral	Available with 50–100% risk	Available 'with exclusion'	Available
Juvenile spinal muscle atrophy	Not available	Not available	Not available

Table 2. Insurance policies for applicants at risk from genetic disorders. Estimation of the applicant's risk of developing a particular genetic disorder is based only on family history

Syndrome	Life insurance	Health insurance	Accident insurance
Huntington's chorea	Not available if a parent and/or a grandparent died from it	Available 'with exclusion'	Not available
Friedreich's ataxia	Available only after 25 years	Available (also before 25 years)	Available
Mucoviscidosis	Available only after 21 years	Available (also before 21 years)	Available
Hereditary hemosiderosis	Available	Available	Available
Muscular dystrophies:			
Duchenne	Available	Available	Available
Facioscapulohumeral	Available	Available	Available
Juvenile spinal muscle atrophy	Available	Available	Available
Celiac disease	Available	Available	Available
Morbus Gaucher	Available	Available	Available
Diabetes mellitus	Available. If more than one first degree relative is affected. Available with risk up to 25%	Available Available 'with exclusion'	Available Available
Psychiatric disorders (suicide, schizophrenia, paranoia)	Available. If more than 2 first degree relatives are affected. Available with risk of 25–50%	Available Available 'with exclusion'	Available Available
Cardiovascular	If more than two first degree relatives are affected, available with risk 25–100%	Available 'with exclusion'	Available

For the other genetic pathologies the applicant may already have developed the disorder at the time of application or his risk of doing so would be suggested by the details of his family history which he is required to furnish with his application. A patient with hereditary hemosiderosis (iron storage defect) would not be accepted for life insurance if there is already liver damage but if not he would be accepted with a risk factor of up to 200%. For health insurance they would be accepted 'with exclusion . . .', and would be accepted for accident insurance at a normal premium. However, normal life, health and accident insurance conditions would be applied for persons whose risk is apparent from their family history. For Gaucher's disease (lipid storage disorder) life insurance would be considered for adult patients (over 20 years) but with a 100–200% risk factor. They would be eligible for health insurance 'with exclusion . . .', they would not be eligible for accident insurance on account of the mental weakness. Persons whose risk is apparent only from their family history would be treated as normal applicants.

Patients with Friedreich's ataxia and those adjudged to be at high risk from the family history may be considered for life insurance only from age 25 onwards. They would be eligible for health insurance 'with exclusion' but not for accident insurance. People at risk of Huntington's chorea would be considered for life insurance once past the age of 60 years, would not be considered before the age of 20 years, but between these ages would be considered with a high risk factor of up to 600%.

Patients with the various muscular dystrophies are unlikely to be considered for any insurance if severely affected, but those forms of late onset and relatively mild expression may be considered for life insurance but with restricted duration and a high risk factor. Generally they would not be considered for health and accident insurance. Persons whose risk is apparent from their family history would be treated as normal applicants. Patients with neurofibromatosis would be considered for life insurance but if the central nervous system is affected there would be an increased risk factor. They would be considered for health insurance 'with exclusion', but would be eligible for accident insurance only if the central nervous system was not affected. Persons whose risk is apparent from their family history would be treated as normal applicants. Mucoviscidosis (cystic fibrosis) patients who survived past childhood would only be eligible for life cover after age 21 but with varying risk factors depending on age and severity of the condition. For those aged 21–35 years the risk factor would be 700%, and after 35 years 300–400%. They would not be eligible for health insurance if severely affected but otherwise would be eligible 'with exclusion'. They would also be eligible for accident insurance. Persons whose risk is apparent from their family history would be insured for life cover only after age 21. Patients with thalassemia minor (heterozygous) would be accepted with a small risk factor for life insurance and for health insurance 'with exclusion'. Those who are heterozygous without any pathological symptoms (thalassemia minima) would be regarded as normal for life and health insurance with normal premiums. Those with thalassemia major (homozygous) would not be considered for life insurance before age 19, but would be eligible after that age with a high risk factor and would be eligible for health insurance 'with exclusion'. All three degrees of thalassemia would be eligible for accident insurance. Patients with phenylketonuria (PKU) would not be considered for life cover before the age of 8–10 years on account of the difficulty of ensuring full dietary control once the child starts school. After the age of 10 years life insurance would carry a risk factor only if some degree of mental subnormality had already become established and such cases would not be eligible for accident insurance, but would receive health insurance 'with exclusion'. An individual requesting life cover who reports diabetes type 1 (juvenile) in her/his family but who is her/himself unaffected, confirmed in the insurance medical examination would be accepted for life cover if no other risk factors were present (overweight, hyperlipidemia, hypertension etc.) but with a factor if that was the case. This risk factor would be increased if the disease was already present and would vary according to its severity. If the applicant already has severe diabetes she/he would not be accepted for life insurance. Depending on the severity of the condition the applicant may or may not be eligible for health insurance 'with exclusion' and for accident insurance. It should be stressed that the restrictions and risk factors given above represent standard values which may be somewhat modified by the insurance MD who considers the applications on an individual basis, and may vary slightly between companies.

This selection of genetic conditions, chromosomal, monogenic and multifactorial, shows that the question of insurance is obviously complex. The selection shows that genetic information is used by the insurers and that the distinction between 'traditional' genetic knowledge and 'new' molecular genetic knowledge is actuarially irrelevant. It is a political decision to forbid the use of knowledge gained by 'new' methods and to allow the use of knowledge gained by 'traditional' methods. The examples illustrate cases where the applicant is affected or is at high risk because of the family history. Modern molecular genetic methods allow those high risk cases to be resolved into a group who will not develop the disorder because they do not have the necessary genes and those who have the genes and therefore have a probability amounting in some cases to virtual certainty that they will.

8.4 CONCLUSION

According to the Austrian genetechnique law information from such tests must neither be requested nor required from the applicant.

> Employers and insurance companies including also their representatives and collaborators are forbidden to obtain, request, take or otherwise use results of gene analyses of their employees, applicants for employment, or for those who wish to insure themselves'.

However, it is clear from the above that it may be to the advantage of the applicant to provide such information. Without it, on the basis of the family history he/she is automatically considered a patient by the insurance company and will pay a premium increased according to the individual risk factor. If the result of the genetic test is positive he/she is in the same position. If, however, it is negative, then the genetic problem is irrelevant, there would be no restriction on the policy and he/she would pay a normal premium. Thus from the economic point of view it may be well worthwhile for the applicant to spend the money for such a test (the insurer does not and must not cover such expenses) and to ask the insurer to accept the voluntary submission of this evidence.

However, this economic argument is only one of many. There is the psychological question of how a positive result would affect the attitude and the outlook of the individual tested, there is the social problem of how it would impinge on the interpersonal relationships of the individual with his/her family, friends, acquaintances, and business colleagues and the 'Gentechnik-Gesetz' is mainly politically inspired.

REFERENCES

Austrian Federal Law 510 (1994) Gene-technique Law-GTG Federal law publication for the Austrian Republic , July 12th, pp. 4111–4150.

Council of Europe (1997) Convention for the Protection of Human Rights and Dignity of the Human Being with regard to the Application of Biology and Medicine: Convention on Human Rights and Biomedicine. *European Treaty Ser.* 164, 1–12.

Harper, P.S. (1993) Insurance and genetic testing. *Lancet* **341**: 224–227.

Hauser, G. and Jenisch, A. (1998) Laws regarding insurance companies. *J. Med. Genet.* **35**: 526–527.

Chapter

9

CLINICAL ASPECTS OF GENETICS AND INSURANCE

The development and roles of Codes of Practice

Sandy Raeburn

Sag, Freund, was ist den Theorie,
Wenn's klappen soll und klapp't noch nie.
Und was ist Praxis, sei nicht dumm,
Wenn's klappt und niemand weiss warum. (*Anonymous*)

9.1 INTRODUCTION

Other chapters of this work have concentrated on the examination of how a balance between actuarial fairness (also known as mutuality in the private insurance market) and social justice (or solidarity between all people in the community) can be struck. There are theoretical models of how to tackle such politically and socially sensitive issues. There are also practical examples, from different countries, of possible legislation. Finding robust solutions is important, because society wishes to provide for those who are disadvantaged by genetic problems, within a system in which private insurers can compete to provide life and health care cover. In the UK this is set within a tax-funded NHS system which provides universal health care. However, cost restraints are raising the possibility of increased rationing by the NHS which may therefore be reduced to core provision. The field of medical genetics is developing so rapidly that there is a strong possibility that present or future laws relating to genetics and insurance might be outdated rapidly. On the other hand, it is important to establish systems to prevent any abuses of genetic information, either by health care providers, insurers or by potential applicants for insurance cover. If any party to a contract has information relevant to that contract, not available to the other parties, there is a considerable danger that unfair agreements will be established, leading to unacceptable risks, unilaterally.

The use of voluntary codes of practice has been successful in a number of areas. Thus geneticists and neurologists agreed that presymptomatic genetic testing for the Huntington's disease gene would follow a rigorous protocol. This approach has been accepted worldwide. Another example, from the UK, is a Code of Practice which the Department of Education has produced, for identifying and assessing special educational needs (Department of Education, 1994). If such codes can be applied without legislation then there could be adequate protection for all parties, in ways which are flexible. Codes of Practice are amenable to development and evolution as knowledge increases. This chapter describes how both clinical geneticists and insurers in the UK have developed standards for handling the interface between genetics and insurance. It also examines exactly what the clinical geneticist does, how this provides support for families with genetic risks and indicates suggestions which families, and the umbrella organization, the Genetic Interest Group, have mentioned to the author about their needs in terms of insurance and other community/social inputs.

Sometimes there is a conflict between theory and practice. Those who espouse theory attempt to consider every possibility and to make decisions which account for all of these; on the other hand practitioners are often too focused on the problems which they have most recently encountered, giving a risk of bias in their decision-making. The German poem introducing this chapter speaks eloquently of the frequent mismatch between theory and practice.

9.2 CLINICAL GENETIC SERVICES

Genetic services have developed variably in different countries of the world and differ considerably even within Europe (Harris, 1997). There are several publications describing the clinical genetic services in the UK (e.g. Harper *et al.*, 1996; Raeburn and Hsu, 1998; Raeburn *et al.*, 1997). When referral to a clinical geneticist takes place (sometimes from primary care and sometimes from other community specialists or hospital), the first essential is that the clinical diagnosis is confirmed. Then, if not obvious from the diagnosis, the mode of inheritance is established. This will facilitate assessment of the genetic risks and awareness by the geneticist of those relatives who may wish genetic counseling. Next, the options available to individuals in the family can be listed, allowing those with increased risks to select their preferred course of action.

9.3 DIAGNOSIS

The clinical geneticist who sees individuals referred with genetic problems is responsible for identifying or confirming the diagnosis. This may be achieved by clinical means. Diagnosis may be obvious in affected members of the family (e.g. those with Huntington's disease); in other instances the specific genetic diagnosis can be very difficult to pinpoint by clinical means (e.g.with rare types of neurogenetic syndrome). Sometimes the family diagnosis is very clear (e.g. a predisposition to breast cancer) but the specific genetic subgroup and therefore the identification of the degree of risk to relatives, can be elusive. Detailed investigation, using molecular genetic tests is increasingly required to confirm or exclude specific single gene conditions. Having done so it is possible to recognize the mode of inheritance and if relatives are at risk. Then, the clinical geneticist can offer all who wish it, appropriate information and counseling. The way in which the at-risk family members are approached is extremely important, particularly to prevent an individual's 'right not to know' from being infringed.

9.4 RISK ASSESSMENT

Geneticists, and their clients with inherited conditions, base a great proportion of the evaluation of illness on an assessment of risks. These can be divided into the risk that someone inherits a gene from their parent and, if so, the risk of that gene causing disease by a particular age. For diseases due to single gene defects the former risk is often simply calculated; because genes and chromosomes are mostly present in an individual in pairs (one copy having been inherited from each parent), the chance of inheriting either one or other is 50%. Thus, in Huntington's disease (HD), where the abnormal gene manifests itself in later adult life in the presence of a normal copy, the risk to offspring of inheriting it is also 50%. The second aspect of risk appraisal, penetrance of the gene, comes into play when an abnormal gene, such as that for HD has been inherited. The penetrance is the likelihood of the individual who carries the gene being affected.

If a healthy person at risk of HD attends a genetic department and requests all relevant information, he/she will be told of the theoretical risk of inheriting the gene and of the possibility of having genetic tests to determine if that has happened or not. Those who wish testing and are subsequently found to be positive for the HD gene, might then ask about the likely age when first symptoms could occur or even of the likely longer-term prognosis.

It is clear that the information that individuals at increased genetic risk often want to know, and which can now be provided in detail by the geneticist, is also relevant to the underwriter and the insurer. Knowledge that a disease gene is present and of its likely penetrance by a given age, affecting that person's prognosis, could impact on life policies and several other types of insurance.

For HD, and several other single gene disorders with effects mainly in later adult life, it is self-evident that genetic test results have a validity for underwriting. For many other disease genes the implications of positive genetic test results are less clear-cut and it will require empirical research over many years to establish each test's validity, either for use in clinical prediction or for underwriting.

9.5 GENETIC COUNSELING

The essential ethos of genetic counseling is to provide accurate information to those who wish this (Harper, 1998). The autonomy of the individual must be respected. This has two effects: firstly, that no-one is presented with information they have not sought out; secondly, that all possible options open to the individual are made available so that she or he can choose that most appropriate, or perhaps request other, quite different possibilities. An interesting effect of offering someone three or four options is that it prompts them to think up other possibilities more acceptable to them. Thus the provision of a list of options is empowering.

In practice the two elements of genetic counseling (nondirectiveness and individual autonomy) are progressed by emphasizing to clients at a genetic clinic that it is their agenda that will be tackled. An approach the author favors is to make out a list of the individual's own questions **before** embarking on all the genetic and other medical information-giving. Also, in many of the UK genetic centers, referred individuals are often visited at home by a genetic nurse specialist, prior to the clinical genetic consultation. In the Nottingham service, over 80% of referred families are first visited at home.

Genetic counseling also involves the provision of appropriate psychosocial support following a confirmed diagnosis, identification of an individual's future risk or testing to identify carriers. The psychosocial support is often carried out by trained genetic nurse specialists or genetic counselors who work within a genetic center but whose involvement with the family begins at the home visit and, develops through the diagnostic and counseling sessions and, often, beyond.

9.6 OPTIONS FOR INDIVIDUALS AND FAMILIES

Even with quite simple genetic situations there can be a variety of options open to affected individuals and their families. *Table 1* summarizes some of these, emphasizing the right not to be informed. Those who wish to find out more can be told first of the theoretical risks; they may wish to leave things at that. However, some will wish to proceed further, asking particularly for genetic tests to show if they are carriers of a gene which might affect either

Table 1. Some options for a person at risk of Huntington's disease

1. To remain uninformed about any degree of risk
2. To delay testing until later in life
3. To decline all testing, for all time
4. To consider prenatal exclusion tests in a future pregnancy
5. To consider preimplantation genetic testing with replacement of unaffected embryos
6. To proceed to being tested for the Huntington's disease gene (after following a planned protocol)

themselves in later life, or future members of their family. This part of the process of genetic counseling and clinical genetic assessment often involves the possibility of undertaking genetic tests which could identify any individual risk more clearly.

The practice of genetic counseling owes a great deal to the person-centered counseling model of Carl Rogers (1951). Considerable experience and skill is required to pass on information about medical aspects and genetics in a way that is clear and authoritative, but without disempowering the individual. An important tool in achieving this is to allow time to pass between the listing of a person's different options and the stage at which they must decide which options to progress. Some options though, such as prenatal diagnosis with the possibility of selective termination of an affected fetus, put particular pressures on the individual; of necessity, such decisions must be made within a critically short time frame.

9.7 THE EXAMPLES OF CANCER GENETICS AND HUNTINGTON'S DISEASE

The major developing element of genetic work is the provision of cancer genetic services in collaboration with site-specific specialists and oncologists. These have particular relevance to insurance because an individual at greater risk of developing cancer will confront self-evident implications about his or her life expectancy or the possibility of morbidity (Meissen and Berchek, 1997). Only a small proportion of people with the common cancers (breast, colorectal or ovary) will have strong single gene predispositions which could be transmitted to relatives, who then have a high risk of being affected by particular cancers. However, media interest has caused the genetic contribution to cancer to be exaggerated even though more than 95% is due to either sporadic causes or to multifactorial causes, in which the familial element is minor. Despite a huge literature in this area over the past five years there are few validated guidelines for selecting the highest risk individual or family. However, all selection and stratification procedures should be achieved within the framework of individual and/or familial autonomy.

Huntington's disease is an example where the model for genetic counseling and presymptomatic genetic diagnosis has been developed, this time with much national and international agreement. There are international guidelines for providing presymptomatic genetic testing. Neurologists and geneticists have agreed not to test individuals under the age of 18 and not to proceed with presymptomatic testing until there has been adequate counseling and psychological preparation for both the testing and the disclosure of the result. Involvement and collaboration of neurologists, psychiatrists and geneticists is appropriate at all stages of the process. Several thousand individuals worldwide have now had such presymptomatic testing (about 40% of whom were found to be positive for the HD gene) with minimal adverse events (e.g. Benjamin *et al.*, 1994; Brock *et al.*, 1989; Holloway *et al.*, 1995; Simpson *et al.*, 1992; Tyler *et al.*, 1992).

9.8 THE ETHOS OF CLINICAL GENETICS: UNWRITTEN CODES OF PRACTICE

As can be seen from the above sections, the clinical geneticist has an ethos which in many respects must be neutral, not forcing his or her views on the individual consultand. There is no written code of practice but the ethos is implied in the curriculum published for training clinical geneticists (Joint Council for Higher Medical Training, 1996).

The work of the clinical geneticist has developed in a different and more patient-centered way compared with the acute medical and surgical specialties or even some chronic specialties, such as neurology. This is because the acute specialties, especially, have a culture of rapid response to emerging situations in which it is impossible to consult exhaustively with an ill person. Thus, the training of nongenetic specialists often emphasizes clear-thinking, decisive action in which the doctor plays the major part in any decision-making. In contrast, the clinical geneticist lays out a menu of options and attempts to empower the individual and the family to choose for themselves. The different approaches of a geneticist might often produce conflict with other specialists, for example surgeons. Interestingly, the clinical geneticist's wish for patient autonomy in decision-making is not at odds with the published Genetics Code of Practice of the Association of British Insurers (ABI, 1997). That Code emphasizes that nobody will be forced to take a genetic test against their wishes. There is no such code for surgical specialists although the principle was recently emphasized in the report of the Advisory Committee on Genetic Testing on late onset disorders (1998). The author's recent (unpublished) observations (as ABI Genetics Advisor) also demonstrate that insurance companies are trying extremely hard to avoid indirect pressure on an individual's decision-making, for example by implying that were a person to take a test and find that it is negative, then the premium would be appropriately reduced.

9.9 GENETIC TEST INTERPRETATION

There are thousands of different genetic diseases; for each, there are a number of different genetic tests possible. Further, an individual may apply for several different types of life or health insurance. Therefore, the process of validating a genetic test already carried out on an individual, for use in connection with that person's insurance application is very complex. The interpretation of genetic tests in individual subjects is also complex and needs to be tackled in the context of the family history and the person's health history. Relevant data from similar groups of individuals, together with appropriate follow-up studies may not be available.

Given these complexities, it is not surprising that misunderstandings between geneticists and insurers have occurred. The HGAC report on Genetics and Insurance noted 'anecdotal evidence' that individuals with genetic diseases perceived that they were unfairly assessed. In my part-time work as genetic advisor to the ABI, it is clear that sometimes problems relate to the geneticist's lack of knowledge of the many insurance options and of how an application is assessed for assignment to a particular insurance pool. There have also been situations in which the insurers misunderstood a family history (e.g. for autosomal dominant conditions with variable phenotype or for multifactorial conditions which were assumed to be dominant, see Chapter 4).

9.10 WHY DO SOME INDIVIDUALS WANT GENETIC TESTS?

The reasons most often quoted to the author are:

- to inform reproductive or other life decisions;
- to institute appropriate preventive measures;
- to increase self-knowledge.

All these reasons, especially the third, are extremely personal (Meissen and Berchek, 1997). This is why geneticists have agreed that they will not pressure anyone to have genetic tests and also why insurers have emphasized in the ABI Code of Practice that they will not require genetic tests to be carried out against the individual's judgment. Insurers wish to be informed of genetic test results already performed on an individual and reported back, so that there is symmetry of information between both parties of the contract.

The insurer's reasons for being informed about the results of genetic tests already carried out will usually mirror the reasons of the individual, especially the first two. Knowing that someone is at greater risk of developing a disease, with an effect on life expectancy, will influence the risk pool to which he/she is assigned. Also, that knowledge might indicate a need for medical/surgical intervention which thus influences the cost of medical expenses insurance. There could also be the possibility of requesting prenatal tests in a pregnancy and claiming that cost from a medical expenses policy. Similarly, the medical need for breast screening or prophylactic mastectomy might be argued, and claimed from private medical insurance.

The UK situation involves an interesting mixture of NHS provision for all individuals and families plus the option of voluntary private medical insurance. It is clear that in terms of applying the principles of evidence-based medicine to decisions about screening or prophylactic operations, the private insurers are already alongside, or leading, the opinions of NHS purchasers of these services (Bull, 1998).

9.11 WHY DO OTHER PEOPLE NOT WISH TO KNOW?

Some members of families with genetic disorders like HD, prefer not to enquire about their risk. This may be due to a great deal of self-knowledge and the awareness that knowing something disturbing about their future health (or death) would, for them, be unacceptable. Perhaps, some others have not appreciated that they can seek further genetic information; their own relatives or doctors may have assumed that it would be wrong to tell them. For further discussion of the many reasons for an individual to make an autonomous decision **not** to be tested, the reader is referred to Richards and Marteau (1996).

The assessment of individual genetic tests for use in insurance can be explored using the principles of Hume's fork (Fieser, 1977).

(i) The genetic test result will either be self-evidently relevant and usable, or not so.
   - A positive test result for the HD gene will usually be very relevant to a person's life expectancy and would influence life insurance contracts.
   - A negative result for the HD gene in a person, who was at increased risk (based on family history), is also relevant. The negative result can lead to normal insurance rates being offered, where, otherwise, there would have been a loading of the premium.
   - A genetic test result showing that an individual is or is not a carrier of cystic fibrosis is of no relevance to the individual's own health insurance history.

(ii) The genetic test result might be relevant, but empirical observations are required to determine this.
   - The use of apolipoprotein E (ApoE) polymorphisms to indicate the risk of an individual developing Alzheimer's disease in an insurance context requires much more data.

- The risk of developing colorectal cancer in an individual who does not have a single gene cause and who has a family history suggesting multifactorial inheritance, may be influenced by certain genetic test results. The exact degree of risk cannot at present be estimated.

Following publication of the Code of Practice, the ABI issued a matrix of genetic conditions to underwriters and Chief Medical Officers, which indicated the insurance relevance of particular tests. Other tests were excluded for insurance usage. The eight conditions (reduced to seven conditions in July 1999) included in that matrix for autosomal dominant disorders were potentially available for service use in the NHS by clinical geneticists. Diseases included on the other two matrices were not so relevant as the conditions were autosomal recessive or X-linked. Either the adult individuals involved would be healthy carriers or they would have manifest the condition in childhood, before the question of insurance applications arose.

The need for empirical research to clarify the insurance relevance of genetic tests in the assessment of multifactorial conditions is now being addressed. Other areas needing empirical studies are familial cancer, the familial aspects of cardiovascular diseases and genetic conditions predisposing to osteoarthritic disease (requiring, for example, hip replacement).

9.12 INSURANCE CODES OF PRACTICE

The ABI Genetics Code of Practice was the first comprehensive document detailing how insurers can cope with the increasingly complex challenges of genetics. Because of the detail, and of the ABI requirement (for continuing membership) that member companies comply with all elements of the Code, monitoring is essential. Initial data over the first months of usage of the Code were extremely promising. The ABI Code of Practice has been described elsewhere in this book (Chapter 7). Other countries, particularly the US and Australia, have attempted to develop genetic codes of practice. Interest, now, centers on the applicability of the ABI Code to other countries.

9.13 CONCLUSION

There is a strong positive relationship between the information some individuals wish to have about their genetic constitution and those data of value in underwriting. Only the high risk situations occurring with major single gene disorders have validity for clinical or insurance use at present. The research data now required to elucidate the genetic component of complex, polygenic disorders could be of great importance in developing initiatives to improve the nation's health. In the future, such research could best be achieved by collaborations between geneticists, insurers, actuaries and epidemiologists.

REFERENCES

ABI (Association of British Insurers) (1997) *ABI Genetics Code of Practice.* Association of British Insurers, London.

Advisory Committee on Genetic Testing (1998) *Genetic Testing for Late Onset Disorders.* ACGT, Department of Health, London.

Benjamin, C.M., Adam, S, Wiggins, J.L. *et al.* (1994) Proceed with care: direct predictive testing for Huntington disease. *Am. J. Hum. Genet.* **55:** 606–617.

Brock, D.J.H., Mennie, M., Curtis, A. *et al.* (1989) Predictive testing for Huntington's disease with linked DNA markers. *Lancet* **i:** 463–466.

Bull, A. (1998) 'Contracting for cancer services'. *Official Proceedings of the International Federation of Health Funds Conference*, Cape Town, 22–26 March, pp. 97–110.

Department of Education (1994) 'Code of Practice on the Identification and Assessment of Special Educational Needs'. Central Office of Information, HMSO, London.

Fieser, J. (1977) *The Hume Archives*. University of Tennessee (accessed via the Internet).

Harper, P.S. (1998) *Practical Genetic Counselling*, 3rd Edn. Butterworth-Heinemann, Oxford.

Harper, P.S., Hughes, H.E. and Raeburn, J.A. (1996) *Clinical Genetics Services into the 21st Century*. A report from the Clinical Genetics Committee of the Royal College of Physicians, London.

Harris, R. (ed.) (1997) Genetic Services in Europe. A comparative study of 31 countries by the concerted action on genetic services in Europe. *Eur. J. Hum. Genet.* **5:**. 188–195.

Holloway, S., Mennie, M., Crosbie, A. *et al.* (1995) Predictive testing for Huntington's disease: social characteristics and knowledge of applicants, attitudes to the test procedure and decisions made after testing. *Clin. Genet.* **46:** 175–180.

Joint Council for Higher Medical Training (1996) Clinical genetic training programme, produced by the Chairman and members of the Specialist Advisory Committee, Royal College of Physicians, London.

Meissen, G.J. and Berchek, R.L. (1997) Intended use of predictive testing by those at risk for Huntington's disease. *Am. J. Med. Genet.* **26:** 283–293.

Raeburn, J.A and Hsu, R. (1998) *Trent Genetics Review*. NHS Executive, Sheffield.

Raeburn, J.A., Kent, A. and Gillott, J. (1997) Genetic services in the UK. *Eur. J. Hum. Genet.* **5**(suppl. 2): 188–195.

Richards, M. and Marteau, T. (1996) *The Troubled Helix*. Cambridge University Press, Cambridge.

Rogers, C.R. (1951) *Client-centred Therapy*. Constable, London (most recent reprint 1990).

Simpson, S.A., Besson, J., Alexander, D., Allan, K. and Johnston, A.W. (1992) One hundred requests for predictive testing for Huntington's disease. *Clin. Genet.* **326:** 326–330.

Tyler, A., Ball, D. and Craufurd, D. (1992) Presymptomatic testing for Huntington's disease in the United Kingdom. *BMJ* **304:** 1593–1596.

Chapter

10

POLICY OPTIONS FOR HEALTH AND LIFE INSURANCE IN THE ERA OF GENETIC TESTING

Tony McGleenan and Urban Wiesing

10.1 INTRODUCTION

Throughout the previous chapters a number of strategies were examined which could be adopted by policy makers both at national and transnational level in order to avoid or ameliorate the potential problems posed for societies reliant on health and life insurance in the era of genetic testing and predictive medicine. These strategies can be subdivided, broadly speaking, into three separate categories. First, there are those policy options which can be regarded as macro responses. These are policies which can only operate given significant structural change within international and governmental practice as well as market behavior. Secondly, there is a category of median responses which will require alterations both to legislation and to industry practice but which do not involve a wholesale restructuring of the common conceptions of the insurance market. Thirdly, and finally, there are a series of possible micro-solutions which offer small-scale changes in the implementation of insurance practices and related legal regulation.

10.2 MACRO SOLUTIONS

10.2.1 Alter the insurance market

The nature of the insurance market within the European Union could be altered by the introduction of legislation which seeks by various means to alter the balance between social and private insurance. At the moment in many European countries there is a reasonably coherent social system of health insurance, although in some states, notably the UK this provision has been reduced for fiscal and ideological reasons. In states with such a generous and well-established social insurance provision it might well prove to be possible to bolster the social insurance system and minimize the importance and impact of the private health insurance system. The same is true also for mixed social and private health insurance systems such as those which exist in Germany, where the private health insurers operate more or less like a social health insurance system. This would not be such a viable option in states where there is not a strong history of social health insurance. The costs involved in constructing such a system are high. The frustration of recent attempts in the USA to introduce a social system of health insurance is instructive. There clearly is in some states an ideological tolerance for uninsurability among large sections of the population. Coupled with the lobbying power of financial institutions such as insurance companies this tolerance severely undermines the likelihood of successfully altering the balance between social and private provision in such states.

On the other hand: the problems posed for life insurance will be quite different and are not related to existing social systems, because there is in most states no social life insurance system. Where there is some state support for life benefits it tends to be extremely limited in scope. The introduction of a social system of life insurance is not a realistic option.

10.2.2 Prohibit the use of genetic information

The prohibition of the use of genetic information could be introduced at a transnational level across an entity like the European Union. Such strategies have already been attempted at a national level as is discussed in Chapters 7 and 8. However, a number of difficulties are evident at that level. The major problem with a prohibition on the use of genetic information by the private insurance industry is the threat of adverse selection. Even the more optimistic models projected by the insurance industry all indicate that a degree of adverse selection will inevitably arise from any prohibition on the utilization of known genetic information for insurance purposes. Furthermore major definitional problems arise from the confusion which surrounds the question of what actually amounts to genetic information. This is apparent from the range of definitions of genetic information outlined in Chapter 8. It is not immediately clear how 'traditional' genetic knowledge as derived from family pedigrees can be distinguished from molecular genetic knowledge and from other prognostic medical information. It is also not clear how we deal with genetic information which was gained by clinical examination with new diagnostic techniques, for example, the information about polycystic kidney disease discovered by ultrasound. The insurance industry already uses genetic information gained from nonmolecular sources in the calculation of individual risk rating. Deriving a conceptual distinction between these practices and the use of the same information obtained in a molecular genetic test is extremely difficult if not impossible. Such a distinction is based on historical and developmental factors rather than any objectively sustainable conceptual difference and is therefore largely an arbitrary one. The important factor is not the methodology used to obtain the information but the potential of that information to predict the future likelihood of an insurance claim. This confusion and the threat of adverse selection may well make any large scale prohibition of the use of genetic information by the European insurance industry unjustifiable and almost totally unworkable.

10.3 MID LEVEL SOLUTIONS

10.3.1 Soft regulation of the insurance market

A full understanding of the need for regulation of the insurance market must begin with the highlighting of an important distinction. This is the difference between requests for the disclosure of existing genetic information and requests for a genetic test before signing an insurance contract. The second issue is relatively unproblematic whereas the first is much more controversial. If the insurer does not ask for a genetic test the 'classical' situation of insurance is maintained. As insurance covers the risks of an unknown future, the most important question is the management of genetic information which is known to the applicant before he proposes for insurance.

Systems of soft regulation are used with increasing frequency in the field of science and biotechnology because of the perceived advantages of operating a flexible nonstatutory form of lawmaking. This approach is prevalently used, for example, in the UK where the field of genetic technology is predominantly regulated by the use of procedural norms. This is also true of the issue of genetics and insurance.

The procedural method of regulation of genetics and insurance has been formalized somewhat in the UK by the response of the government to the HGAC report. As outlined in Chapter 7 the government broadly welcomed the HGAC recommendations although significantly did not accept the idea of a continued general moratorium. In April 1999 the Department of Health established the Genetics and Insurance Committee which has the following terms of reference:

> to develop and publish criteria for the evaluation of specific genetic tests, their application to particular conditions and their reliability and relevance to particular types of insurance.

Clearly the structures developed in the UK represent a highly reflexive and responsive mode of regulating genetics and insurance without developing binding norms. This approach would be difficult to adopt in states where such statutory prohibitions have already been enacted.

10.3.2 Industry self-regulation

Closely allied to the notion of industry moratoria is that of self-regulation. This strategy presupposes a degree of trust and responsibility on the part of the industry in question. Such a situation has developed in the United Kingdom where, shortly after the publication of the HGAC report, the ABI, an organization representing 95% of insurance companies in the UK, published a new Code of Practice for genetics and insurance (see section 7.3.6).

The Code of Practice adopted by the ABI in the UK is interesting *per se*, but the more important issue, from the perspective of an appraisal of general policy options, is whether self-regulation is, in general, an acceptable means of responding to the challenges posed by predictive genetic information. There are obvious problems with relying on self-regulatory systems. There is a wealth of experience in the UK with the problems posed by allowing privatized utilities to operate systems of self-regulation. The results in many of these cases have been less than satisfactory because of the self-evident problems which exist when there is no external sanction imposed on a financially powerful institution.

10.3.3 Moratoria

The adoption of voluntary moratoria on the use of genetic testing has been a widespread response of the insurance industry throughout Europe. In Germany, France, the Netherlands and the UK organizations representing the interests of the insurance industry have announced that they will voluntarily refrain from requesting the results of genetic tests for a period of years. The attractions of this strategy for the insurance industry, at least in the short term, are not difficult to discern. From the perspective of public relations it enables the insurance industry to appear sensitive to public concerns and responsive to criticism. Moratoria also afford an industry time in which to formulate a desired response to a particular challenge. This option also has a prestige enhancing effect for an industry in so far as it reflects a strong sense of moral responsibility on the part of the industry in question. In reality, it may well be the case that the current round of moratoria are not such a major concession to public opinion given that there are very few actuarially relevant and accurate genetic tests available. In the UK the moratorium is itself limited to policies which do not exceed a value of £100 000. The argument advanced for this is that in the UK, life insurance can be regarded as a primary social good in so far as it is regularly used to support the purchase of property. For proposals in excess of £100 000 the moratorium does not apply. This strategy reveals a careful balancing of the public-relations need not to be seen to deny access to a primary social good and the internalization by the insurance industry of a certain level of risk. When tests which can yield information which will be of value in underwriting begin to appear then the credibility of insurance industry moratoria may come under serious scrutiny. There are, however, also positive advantages to such a system. In an area which is as fast moving as genetic technology there is a need for responsive regulatory frameworks which can rapidly reflect changing circumstances. Moratoria can fulfill this need but the ad hoc nature of these arrangements is undoubtedly a weakness. What, if any, sanctions can be imposed on a company, or indeed a national industry, which chooses to violate the terms of the moratorium? If, for example, one insurance company decides to offer risk-rated insurance at highly competitive rates for those who voluntarily take a genetic test, will other companies be able to resist this challenge? It seems likely that moratoria will only persist as a means of responding to the challenges of genetics and insurance until the actuarial implications of particular genetic profiles can be determined and for as long as all insurance companies faithfully adhere to the moratorium. In the UK adherence to the ABI Code of Practice is a condition of ABI membership. However, 5% of insurance companies do not belong to the ABI. If market advantage can be gained by such a minority of insurance companies by departing from the self-regulatory norms then this mode of regulation may prove to be of reduced utility.

10.3.4 Ceiling systems

The ceiling system of regulating genetic testing in insurance is one which is most commonly associated with the Netherlands. In fact, this approach has been adopted in a number of European countries in response to genetic testing, but has also long been a more general feature of medical testing and life insurance. A system which triggers requests for disclosure or examination is already well established for certain insurance products.

Sandberg, in an extensive analysis of the Dutch option, argues that the value of this strategy is that it subsidizes solidarity and prevents the creation of insurance products which are targeted at those who are not known to be at high risk for genetic diseases. He also highlights the potential weakness of such a system. First, if such a strategy is adopted the ceiling must be set at an equitable level. Secondly, insurers must guard against the possibility of individuals purchasing multiple policies below the threshold level. One method of doing this is to investigate the possibility of multiple purchase at the time of any claim and to regard any concurrent policy as nondisclosure making the insurance contract voidable. Another method would be the development of an information system shared between all the insurance companies. Thirdly, there is also the possibility that some insurance companies may seek to create a niche market by selling risk-rated policies which are actually cheaper than the threshold limited community-rated policy. As Sandberg points out the Dutch system is not 'self-interest optimal' for most purchasers of insurance and so strong regulatory measures must be put in place to prevent market forces undermining the solidarity the system generates.

10.3.5 National legislation

Chapter 7 examined the legislative options which have developed in Europe and beyond in response to the challenges of genetics and insurance and Chapter 8 illustrates the results in one particular state. A number of European states have enacted legislation which specifically addresses the issue of using genetic information in underwriting. Others have legislation which is designed to protect privacy or enhance autonomy through informed consent requirements which also impact on the issue of genetics and insurance. One obvious problem with the response of national legislation is that there is not necessarily any consistency in either the detail or the underlying principles and philosophy of the various laws. In the European context this is obviously a problem. The insurance industry tends to operate as a transnational body yet it is subject to highly individualized legislative regimes in national markets. This situation will almost inevitably create anomalies and differentials. Some states such as Belgium do not permit the use of genetic information even when it is in the applicant's favor. Such individuals may well decide to seek their insurance coverage in a market where their genetic profile can be turned to financial advantage.

On the other hand the attraction of an approach based on individual national laws is that it would take cognisance of the fact that the European insurance market is not a homogenous entity. Alongside the variation in health insurance even in the context of life insurance, which, broadly speaking, is considered a secondary social good in most European states, there are subtle and important differences between member state markets. For example, in the United Kingdom, life insurance premiums are considerably cheaper than they are in other European countries. Since the profit margins on such insurance products are generally speaking lower then there will be an increased incentive on the part of underwriters to engage in a high degree of risk-rated underwriting.

10.3.6 Altering the disclosure laws

Although it is generally stated that the insurance industry operates according to the principle of *uberrimae fides* in relation to the formation of insurance contracts, closer scrutiny reveals significant variation between different states as to the precise nature of the disclosure which must take place in order for a contract to be validly formed. In the United Kingdom, the applicant must disclose all information which the *insurer* would consider to be material to the classification of risk. In countries such as Belgium the standard for disclosure is that which a reasonable insured would have considered material to the risk. In Finland and Switzerland, the duty which is imposed on a proposer is simply to make a reasonable response to questions which are put by the insurer. In France, a system of proportionality is operated whereby claim payments are reduced in proportion to the level of risk which was concealed by a proposer. Perhaps, given the complex and definitionally confused nature of genetic testing an appropriate approach to disclosure would be to place the onus of investigation on the insurer subject to the caveat that the policy is voidable where there has been wilful concealment by the applicant. At the very least a reasonable case can be made for harmonization of approach to this essential element of insurance in regions which claim to operate a single market.

10.4 MICRO SOLUTIONS

10.4.1 Developing insurance products

It has been suggested that the emergence of widely used genetic predictive medicine techniques will ultimately lead to the destruction of the insurance industry. However, a more reasoned argument is that it is much more likely that widespread use of genetic testing will simply lead to a different kind of insurance market where products are specifically tailored to meet the challenges posed by predictive medicine. The areas of critical illness insurance, permanent health insurance, and long-term care insurance are likely to be among those where significant alterations in the insurance products offered will be made.

It is also possible that there will be an expansion of the use of 'with profits' insurance. Individuals pay a premium which will more than cover the risk they bring to the fund. The excess funds are then invested. If the proposer has, in fact, engaged in antiselection, then the detrimental impact on the insurance fund will be reduced by the excess premiums which will be paid. This risk to the insurance fund is therefore externalized to the policyholders. If the individual does not make a claim then the sum paid in excess of the 'premium' can be paid out as a term bonus once a certain number of years have elapsed.

10.4.2 Preinsurance testing

One small-scale intervention which might alleviate some of the potential difficulties of genetics and insurance might be to require that those who are about to take a genetic test sign a type of life or health insurance contract in advance of actually taking the test. This might be a practical solution for some individuals who are part of a 'high risk' group and who are conscious that they do have an already increased likelihood of suffering from a genetic disease. One unfortunate aspect of this is that those who know they have an increased risk of genetic disease will quite possibly already have a family pedigree which will alert underwriters to this fact and will result in an increased premium in any event.

Another approach to this might be a law which makes it illegal to perform a genetic test on an individual who does not already have a valid life or health insurance policy. If the prospective testee does not produce the relevant insurance policy documents to the physician in question then any genetic test performed will amount in law to an assault and the physician/hospital will be liable in damages to the individual. An imaginative twist to such a policy might be a requirement that in the event of a genetic test being performed without the relevant documents the hospital in question should be required to cover the future health care costs of the individual who has been tested without possession of the relevant insurance documents.

The last two policies have a serious disadvantage. They provide a strong disincentive to the taking of genetic tests, even where those tests may provide helpful information for the patient and for the treatment of a disease. This disincentive may mean that a medically useful diagnostic measure will be impeded.

10.4.3 Pretesting insurance

A related possibility is that the insurance market itself might generate a partial solution to the problem by developing an insurance policy which is specifically tailored to those who are about to take a genetic test. The proposer could take out a policy which protected them against the adverse effects of acquiring actuarially relevant prognostic molecular information. This type of insurance on insurance is already operated in the sphere of motor insurance where individuals can take out an insurance policy to protect their 'no-claims' bonus. A derivative of this strategy could be fashioned in order to address the specific problem of predictive genetic information.

10.4.4 Disclosure of definite genetic information

It is possible to develop a system whereby the applicant has to disclose known information about a genetic disease only when the phenotypic onset of the disease will be within a certain limited period of time, for example, five years. This has been recommended for example by the Enquete Commission of the

German Bundestag. The applicant is not required to inform the insurer about dispositions to other diseases. One problem with this approach which makes it hard to implement is that it is of course difficult to predict the phenotypic onset of many diseases in a particular single case. In the individual patient these prognostic evaluations are always likely to be somewhat inaccurate.

In a similar model the applicant has only to inform the insurer about serious diseases. Information about minor genetic diseases or predisposition for diseases with minor implications for the insurer do not have to be disclosed. The difficulty with this approach however is similar to that of the proposal mentioned before: in many cases it may prove difficult to distinguish between these various categories of diseases. The rationale behind this option is the limitation of the financial burdens of adverse selection for the insurer.

In another possible option the applicant does not have to disclose information about certain diseases which have acquired or have been granted a special public status. Such a practice is already operated in some states in relation to some infectious diseases which do not have to be reported to the health authorities because of fears about the generation of disincentives which deter potential sufferers from seeking medical help. Similarly, some diseases which are associated with certain lifestyles are particularly protected by society. This presents particular problems because it requires society to make distinctions between certain diseases and their related lifestyles, a practice that is usually avoided for good reason.

10.5 CONCLUSION

It is apparent that there is a significant variety of options to the problems posed for life and health insurance by the use and acquisition of predictive molecular information. It is most likely that the solutions we have categorized as mid level and micro level will be adopted as the responses to this problem in the European countries although a lot of practical difficulties have to be managed. The macro solutions which have been outlined are much less likely to be adopted because of their enormous political and economic impact. The simple fact of the diversity of the different possible responses presented here suggests that it is quite likely that a combination of these different responses will be used with all the attendant difficulties of striking the appropriate balance between them. Therefore, at least one prognosis is certain: further scrutiny of the technological development in genetics must be matched with continuing detailed analysis of public policy on insurance.

INDEX